The Columbus Affair.
Imperatives for an Italian/ American Agenda

ANTHONY JULIAN TAMBURRI

CASA LAGO PRESS
NEW FAIRFIELD, CT

Spuntini
Volume 1

This book series is dedicated to publishing those studies that are longer than the traditional journal-length essay and yet shorter than the traditional book-length manuscript. Intellectually, it is a light meal, a snack of sorts that holds you over for the full helping that comes with either lunch or dinner.

In memory of Paul Colilli,
in the quest for knowledge and understanding

&

For Michael Dante,
as Winterhawk, and speaker of Blackfoot

COVER ART: Jose María Obregon
Museo Nacional de Arte de México

ISBN 978-1-955995-00-9
Library of Congress Control Number: Available upon request

CASA LAGO PRESS
New Fairfield, CT

TABLE OF CONTENTS

ACKNOWLEDGEMENTS

As I have repeatedly stated in other venues, no essay or book, however small, is ever completed in a vacuum; there is always someone with whom we all share our ideas and inevitably who serves as our sounding board.

A few people have been instrumental in this case. As always, Maria afforded me the time to write. I extend, first, my appreciation to the editors of the books and websites that have hosted previous articulations in which some of this material has already appeared. With regard to those whom I have engaged in conversation, both formally and informally, as well as those who have read one or more of the few previous drafts of this *white book*, I would like to acknowledge the following friends and colleagues: Jerome Bongiorno, Marylou Bongiorno, Ryan Calabretta-Sajder, Stephen Cerulli, Donna Chirico, William Connell, Fred Gardaphé, John Kirby, Rosaria Musco, Mark Pietralunga, Laura Ruberto, Joseph Sciame, Joseph Sciorra, Sabrina Vellucci, John Viola, Antonio Vitti, and Leslie Wilson.

I sincerely thank them all for their keen insights and commentary, whereas any real and/or perceived fallacies are my own.

PREFACE

As Americans we have little understanding how our local holidays evolved into national celebrations. We also tend to see their purpose as being the same from their origins to their implementation to their current practice. However, when a figure, like Christopher Columbus, represents so many things to so many, it should be a signal that his holiday has a long and perhaps hidden history that is distinct from the historical figure. Such a history often reveals more about the society behind the promotion of the holiday, than the people who choose to celebrate it.

Anthony Tamburri's *The Columbus Affair* tackles the Christopher Columbus trilogy (man, myth and legend) spiritually, culturally, and historically. He contextually navigates the ancient world and the modern one to help inform his readers about the historical Columbus as well as the fictional one that serves as both hero and villain. A true Columbus, he argues, lies outside of our 21st century imaginations.

Professor Tamburri also skillfully addresses several key questions and issues in defining the Italian American agenda. He makes a strong case for an Italian American think tank that will explore the dimensions of what has been recognized as Italian American culture. By centering his framework around Christopher Columbus, Professor Tamburri is able to ask, "What defines an Italian American and an Italian in the mind of Americans of Italian ancestry?" His discoveries are unpredictable and equally complex. He furthers this conversation by articulating the role that the Columbus legacy plays in the formation of the New World and the United States. This methodology reveals our limited historical knowledge on the advent of the age of discovery and sheds new light on Columbus's mission in context of the rise of the Spanish Empire. It also provides evidence for both sides of the contemporary Columbus debate on the impact of his voyages. Ultimately, through the fulcrum of Columbus, Professor Tamburri engages in an insightful and provocative discussion on the breadth of the Italian American experience.

The Columbus Affair further advances defining Italian American identity. With Columbus and his four voyages at the core of his academic debate, Anthony Tamburri explores how a Genoan/Genovese navigator working for Spain became an American, Italian American and Italian hero. Through a combination of historical, religious, political, cultural and linguistic lenses, the professor looks at the history of the age of exploration, the legacy of the voyages, and the development of the Columbus holiday. He posits a dissection of traditional socio-political positions. And, his analysis reveals that there are specific differences that must be considered in developing any argument about the legitimacy of our concepts of ethnic heroism. Professor Tamburri discovers how our education of Columbus's mission, accomplishments, and failings translate into our current understandings of Italian and Italian American identity. The monograph reveals how the history of the moment differs from the interpretation of the past. Professor Tamburri has crafted *The Columbus Affair* for all audiences. He triumphs demonstrating how Columbus emerges as a complex symbol in a contentious period of American history.

Leslie Wilson
Professor of History
Associate Dean
College of Humanities and Social Sciences
Montclair State University

INTRODUCTION

The challenge of modernity is to live without illusions and without becoming disillusioned. I'm a pessimist because of intelligence, but an optimist because of will.

ANTONIO GRAMSCI

A s should be apparent to the reader as s/he embarks on this verbal, zig-zag journey with me, the Columbus Affair, as I call it here within, is more complex than some make it out to be. There are those who have presented an historical discussion and have succeeded, as best one could, in the maintenance of an apparent neutrality. There are those, in turn, who are pro-Columbus and have gone all out with a series of declarations that, oft times, are not, or perhaps cannot be, substantiated by history. Finally, there are others still who have made the argument for the elimination of Christopher Columbus for any type of commemoration given what we know about him and the legacies of his voyages to the New World.

For this first group, I have in mind the book by Timothy Kubal, *Cultural Movements and Collective Memory: Christopher Columbus and the Rewriting of the National Origin Myth* (2009), as well as William Connell's "Who's Afraid of Columbus?" (2013).[1] Another essay in this group is Bénédicte Deschamps's "Italian-Amer-

---

[1] Connell later contextualizes the issue in his essay (2018, 17-41) that opens the collection he co-edited with Stanislao Pugliese, *The Routledge History of Italian Americans.*

icans and Columbus Day: A Quest for Consensus Between National and Group Identities, 1840–1910." These three essays, among others, discuss the issue at hand without taking a clear stance either way. Others, in turn, do, and we shall engage those as well.

With regard to the defenders of Columbus, in turn, one cogent argument from this second group, albeit brief, can be found in the few pages Anne Paolucci dedicates to the Columbus Affair in her essay "Preserving the Future Through the Past (A Personal Assessment)" (2007). There, she underscores the importance of history and the need for pro-Columbus people to accept such historical facts, as ugly as they may seem, and only then come to terms with how one might defend Columbus. This is one of the issues I address herein; namely, what are the challenges for those who wish to save Columbus from the trash heap of history. Many other essays, unfortunately, do not adhere to the notion that history is sometimes unpleasant, that the history of conquest, as Paolucci declares, is "an ugly truth" (16). Some of the more popular books in favor of Columbus seem to ignore this aspect of history in general, let alone the specificities of the late fifteenth-century discovery of the New World and all that it pertains.

Finally, there are those who eschew any sort of commemoration of Christopher Columbus as symbol of reverence for Italian Americans. As shall become apparent, Laura Ruberto and Joseph Sciorra debunk the myth that "the majority of working poor Italian

immigrants" were "driving the Columbus enterprise."
In like fashion, Fred Gardaphé underscores Ruberto
and Sciorra's contention that Columbus was not for
the working-class immigrant; he "was never taught
that Columbus had been a symbol of [his] Italian
American identity. [He] was never taught that [his]
family's immigration history mattered enough to be
studied." This state of not knowing — not knowing
the value of one's own ethnic identity; not knowing
the history of the issue at hand, be it Columbus or
other matters — is what Paolucci underscores when,
even in her defense of Columbus, she states that Italian Americans need to accept historical facts no matter how ugly they may be. This historical lacuna is
what Gardaphé also critiques when he states: "[the]
problem is that most don't know how or why [Co-
lumbus] became a part of what some see as Italian
American history. To understand this issue better I
suggested we begin by educating ourselves enough
to make valid arguments that defend whatever interpretation we choose."[2]

---

[2] The one book I do not engage but I wish to note is Djelal Kadir's
*Columbus and the Ends of the Earth: Europe's Prophetic Rhetoric as
Conquering Ideology*; for no other reason than I wish to remain
within an Italian/American framework that is, admittedly, herein limited. In Kadir's study, there is no doubt that Columbus
belongs to that group of Europeans who exploited the Millennial
Vision of the new world in order to further their conversion and
conquest of Native Americans, in our case. See Leonard Sweet's
1986 essay for more on Columbus and the Millennial Vision.

These and other voices with whom I shall engage in this intellectual, crisscrossing zigzag of a quagmire that is the Columbus Affair all demonstrate the major complexities of such argumentation. My goal, modest it may seem, is to examine aspects of each side with the hopes of spurring on an even greater discussion among all parties within our Italian/American semiosphere.[3] After all, one of numerous issues with which Italian Americans at large need to come to terms is the Columbus Affair. Education, philanthropy, social and cultural activism are just three other issues that reside on the same plane. There is an interconnection here the sight of which we cannot lose.

Buona lettura!

---

[3] A technical term within the world of semiotics, by semiosphere I mean that world of notions, ideas, concepts, and their representational forms — words, sounds, visual objects — that we all share to a certain degree and hence allow us to communicate in a functional manner.

PRELIMINARY THOUGHTS

So here he is today, today at last,
riding atop his bright Santa Maria,
the navigator of the *gente mia*,
light of my future, darkness of his past,

the one who comes to dig (for dig we must)
for the high glory of the subway tracks,
the immigrant who died and yet still lacks
identity with his American dust.

> Joseph Tusiani
> "Columbus Day in New York"

i found christopher columbus hiding in the ash tray
what are you doing there, if you please
no one smokes, he said, leave me alone
so i brought him a little soup
i would sit next to him reading a book
until he fell asleep
it was the house arrest that befalls even good people
when they grow old and cannot do anything
he's useless now but he's still yours

> Robert Viscusi
> "An Oration upon the Second Death of
> Christopher Columbus"

The notions, ideas, and interpretations herein have their origins in a series of emails I first sent, as Dean of the John D. Calandra Italian American Institute, to some pro-Columbus people over a two-week period that extended from June to July 2020. Said emails were met with a deafening silence, yet there continued some murmuring about the three-year-old decision of the Calandra Institute's stance of neutrality (Tamburri 2017c) — such murmuring was never directly communicated; as a sort of stage-whisper, it found its way to us. Said stance, I underscore once more here, is radically based on the fact that the Calandra Institute is funded primarily by the State of New York with tax-levied monies; no less than ninety-five percent of our annual budget derives from such funds. What this means is that, organically, our funding originates from a state-wide population of people who represent a plethora of ideas, ideologies, and diverse notions. As such, then, we felt, and continue to do so today, compelled by a sense of fiduciary responsibility. Such rationale, I can only presume, is an anathema to those whose budgets do not depend on tax-levied funding.

Hence, in August, after more than a month of silence since my last email communiqué to the group, I decided to expand on the issues that I had included in the above-mentioned emails. What now follows is my expansion of both various and varying ideas as I crisscross through this imbroglio that I have dubbed the Columbus Affair. It is a quagmire of contrasting thoughts of historical narratives that forces one to travel hither and yon in a chronological zigzag in search of some semblance of resolution, an endnote, however fleeting and unstable said verdict might appear.

My attempt at a forensic argumentation is based on my own intellectual grounding in both Italian studies and Italian/American[2] (read, also, diaspora)

---

[2] My use of the slash (/) in place of the hyphen (-) dates back to an earlier essay of mine (1991).

studies — literature and cinema, as disciplines, and language pedagogy, a field unto itself — that is then informed by a significant dose of semiotics and cultural studies.[3] That said, while my language may sometimes seem specialistic or, as some might say, *jargonistic*, I simply have to presume, and indeed gladly so, that my general reader, who is not an *academic*, is nonetheless an informed one, someone able, and ready, to discern what I intend herein, even though a term or two may seem a bit offshore.

---

[3] My notion of cultural studies follows those concepts that Mas'ud Zavarzadeh and Donald Morton promote in their book (1991).

A CASE IN POINT

In an article published in the *La gazzetta italiana* of Akron, Ohio, John Vallillo and Pam Dorazio Dean report on the name change of Columbus Day to Italian American Heritage and Culture Day, which took place on June 29, 2020. The vote was 12 to 1 to "keep the day as a celebration of Italian American traditions and to rename the second Monday of October 'Italian American Heritage and Culture Day'." In so doing, the special committee set up by the City Council wanted "to remove this issue from the agenda in Akron forever and to move on to other challenges in the community."

So, while the official name of the second Monday in October is no longer to be Columbus Day at the local level in Akron, Ohio, Italian Americans nonetheless could continue to celebrate "the accomplishments of Christopher Columbus ... and the annual cotillion, mass and luncheon, as well as the individual club activities, could continue." It is a sort of have your cake and eat it too, depending on one's perspective; it might also be seen as a total defeat if one's view is to keep Columbus *at all costs*. This second view notwithstanding, it is surely an alternative to the more strident and, at times, seemingly intransigent and truculent stance of "Columbus Do or Die!" To this end, in fact, the Council of the City of Akron resolved as follows:

Section 2. That Council encourages other gov-
ernmental bodies, businesses, organizations, and
public institutions to similarly *recognize the second Monday in October as Italian-American Heritage and Culture Day,* rather than Columbus Day
*without infringing on the rights of the Italian-Amer-
ican community to continue its traditions and celebrations.* (emphasis textual)

Though not overtly articulated in the resolution, the
"the rights of the Italian-American community" clearly include the celebration of "Columbus Day."

In that same article, Vallillo and Dean report that
with the "passing of the resolution four objectives
were accomplished":

1. Acknowledge the Italian-American community's emphasis on celebrating Columbus Day
   as part of our long term history;
2. Acknowledge the contributions of our immigrant ancestors and current Akron and Summit
   County Italian-Americans to local society in
   business, education, art, government and other
   occupations;
3. Acknowledge the strong presence of the Italian-
   American clubs and societies as well as the hun-
   dreds of thousands of dollars contributed to
   scholarships and charitable contributions; and
4. End the assault on Columbus Day by outside
   organizations and local politicians once and for
   all.

The fourth accomplishment, I suspect many would agree, is more of a desired outcome rather than an actual resolution of any facet of the issue at hand.[4] It actually begs two questions rather than guarantee the articulated objective: First, is it not too early to know if potential assaults on Columbus Day will cease?; and second, What does prevent other members of non-Italian-American 'organizations and local politicians' to decide otherwise in the future? This, of course, is speculation on my part at this juncture, and, as such, we should leave it for another time and place. In this venue, instead, I wish to articulate some thoughts on where we are, how we might move forward, and what might be an end point, however fleeting it might appear to some on either side of the Columbus Affair today.

---

[4] "Aspirational" is an adjective that became much more popular with all of its semantic vagaries, during the period of COVID-19; a term for many, one might say, who seem to have wandered (and wondered) aimlessly as the United States dealt with the onslaught of the disease.

TALKING POINTS

What I shall do in this venue is take three of the City of Akron's four objectives, modify them for a more general discussion, and, accordingly, offer some commentary.

1. ACKNOWLEDGE COLUMBUS DAY as a long-time historical symbol for Italian Americans and that its relevance was born from the attempts of people such as Angelo Noce and Carlo Barsotti to "[h]igh-light… Columbus as an Italian progenitor of the United States" and thus "reconfigure the dominant perception of Italian immigrants by associating them with characteristics connoting formality, sophistication, and noblesse."[5]

Until 1892 Columbus was, for all practical purposes, an "American" hero; he had no ethnic hue! Since his initial arrival, it had taken three hundred years for him to be celebrated in North America. In 1792, to be precise, Columbus was hailed "as an appropriate hero and symbol for people who were beginning to see themselves as 'Americans,' not just

---

[5] In their essay on Columbus monuments, Ruberto and Sciorra dedicate an entire section to the crafting of Columbus as an Italian hero (68-73). The two citations above are from pages 70 and 71. Some have also hypothesized an attempt by the U.S. government to acknowledge the 1891 lynchings in New Orleans, LA, as well as the then systemic mistreatment of Italian immigrants, and hence an unstated apology on the part of the U.S. at that time.

Europeans in America," as journalist Clarence Page told us back in 1991.[6] It was the new generation of the native-born Europeans who first embraced Columbus as such. He became "Italian" in 1892, many contend, in a presumed attempt by President Harrison to remedy, if one could, the lynching of eleven Italians the year before in New Orleans. But we do know, as we saw above, that there was a much more concerted effort by Italian *prominenti* themselves to change the general perception of Italians from working class immigrants to a population of a more sophisticated lot. This is a significant point in how Columbus became "Italian"; one can readily begin to understand this more fully by consulting the research on the matter.[7] In his *Cultural Movements and Collective Memory*, Timothy Kubal spells out in detail the social and political phenomena that contributed to the construction of a

---

[6] Ralph Waldo Emerson had sung Columbus's praises in an essay entitled "Self-Reliance" (first published in 1841) and once more in "English Traits" (first published in 1856) through his excoriation of Amerigo Vespucci: "Strange, that the solid truth-speaking Briton should derive from an impostor. Strange, that the New World should have no better luck, — that broad America must wear the name of a thief. Amerigo Vespucci, the pickle-dealer at Seville, who went out, in 1499, a subaltern with Hojeda, and whose highest naval rank was boatswain's mate in an expedition that never sailed, managed in this lying world to supplant Columbus, and baptize half the earth with his own dishonest name. Thus, nobody can throw stones. We are equally badly off in our founders; and the false pickle-dealer is an offset to the false bacon-seller" (604).

[7] Also, pertinent here are studies by Peter Vellon (2014) and Danielle Battisti (2019).

"pan-ethnic Italian American identity" (103) that would eventually lead to Columbus becoming the ethnic sign *par excellence* for and of Italian Americans, thus transforming, as Kubal states, "the national origin myth into an ethnic collective memory" (103).

A speedy way to access this history is to consult two shorter essays that speak to this issue of Italian/American identity and Columbus: one by Benedicte Deschamps (2001), which predates, and another — the above-cited essay by Ruberto and Sciorra — which post-dates Kubal. Deschamps, in fact, tells us:

> The elaboration of the myth of Columbus as the Founding Father of America — which Washington Irving had largely contributed to with the publication of his biography of the Genoan sailor in 1831 — was the key to the rehabilitation of Italian immigrants. In the 1890s, while congressman Henry Cabot Lodge defended the Literacy Test project on the ground that southern Europeans belonged to those "races whose traditions and inheritances, whose thoughts and whose beliefs are wholly alien to ours and with whom we have never assimilated or even been associated in the past," C. A. Barattoni, the vice president of the Executive Committee of the Christopher Columbus Monument, praised the common heritage of Italians and Americans:
>
> > [T]he Italians of this City have thought it appropriate ... to perpetuate the memory

> of that great genius, CHRISTOPHER
> COLUMBUS, a humble son of Italy, but
> to whom America owes its discovery....
> (Deschamps 2001, 127-128)

From Washington Irving's myth of Columbus as the Founding Father of America to the identification of Columbus as "Italian," and hence representational for Italians and Italian Americans, is succinctly offered by Deschamps. As detailed as his account is on Columbus and Italian Americans — an entire chapter dedicated to a detailed narrative — oddly, Kubal does not cover Barattoni and his involvement as vice president of the Executive Committee of the Christopher Columbus Monument. Hence, Deschamps's reference to what we might call Barattoni's act of prestidigitation is fundamental, since he was one of the many *prominenti* whom Ruberto and Sciorra discuss further in their essay:

> The symbolic linking of Italian Americans with Columbus was not a mass effort but rather the project of a small group of economic, political, and culturally elite immigrants. These *prominenti* ('prominent ones') situated themselves between the often-undereducated working poor and Italian government officials and U.S. elites but in reality 'concerned themselves almost totally with their own welfare, prestige, and public image'.... The rememoration of some contemporary Italian Americans often focuses on their working-class immi-

grant ancestors donating pennies to various Columbus projects, disregarding the reality that the few *prominenti*, self-proclaimed ethnic leaders, not the majority of working poor Italian immigrants, were driving the Columbus enterprise. (69)

Ruberto and Sciorra engage here in what Mas'ud Zavarzadeh and Donald Morton have coined a "critical studies" approach. Not merely descriptive, cultural studies, Zavarzadeh and Morton tell us, must also be "critical." As such, it must be more than the "mere description of cultural emergents that aims to give voice to the 'experience' of those who have been denied a space to talk." In their clarification, Zavarzadeh and Morton describe what they distinguish as "dominant" or "experiential cultural studies," which "offers a 'description' of the exotic 'other' and thus provides the bourgeois reader with the pleasure of contact with difference."[8] Instead, for them, critical cultural studies "is not a description but an explanation, not a testimonial but an intervention: it does not simply 'witness' cultural events, but takes a 'position' regarding them" (8). As Zavarzadeh and Morton, underscore, change is the operative word. For them, critical cultural studies should constitute "an articulation of the cultural real that will change the conditions which have blocked those voices from talking"

---

[8] For Zavarzadeh and Morton, the proponents of the dominant cultural studies include the likes of John Fiske and Constance Penley.

(8). The analytical act of the "articulation of the cultural real" in Ruberto and Sciorra's essay brings attention to the fact that "the majority of working poor Italian immigrants" were not "driving the Columbus enterprise" with regard to a popular, mythic narrative that has resisted the passage of time over the past century and one-half. The debunking of any popular, mythic narrative is a responsibility for all Italian Americans who engage in some form of activism, be they on the left or on the right, be they pro- or anti-Columbus. We need to be more informed and eschew all those feel-good anecdotes such as "my grandparents came to America because they wanted to become American, learn English, and be a patriotic citizen!" This counters the factual narrative that of the approximately 4,200,000 who first came to the United States from Italy during the four-plus decades of mass immigration (1880-1924), up to fifty percent retuned.

All three of these studies add to the requisite construction of a larger historical narrative on the Columbus story vis-à-vis Italian Americans. Be one pro- or anti-Columbus, one needs to know the origins of the myth — yes, that *national* myth that became *ethnic* — to be able to make an intelligently informed decision about Columbus Day, its symbolism, and the impact such a semiotic phenomenon that is the sign /Columbus/ can have. Specifically, how does one conceptualize (read, also, interpret) the name (read, also, sign) Columbus? In this brief expose that follows I am relying on notions brought forth by the logician

/ semiotician Charles Sanders Peirce. In his general notion of the sign, Peirce tells us that a sign is something that stands for something to someone. While the sign is, *in principio*, objective, it is, *in termino*, subjective, as the following graph demonstrates:

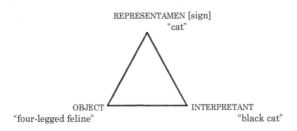

As we can see, the word "cat" (representamen) conjures up the notion of four-legged feline, hence a general notion of the word / sign "cat" (object). It is the next step where one's reaction to the sign /cat/ becomes individual (read, also personal). Peirce's interpretant is dependent on one's personal experiences, choices, desires, and the like. For one person the personal mental image might be a black cat, for another person it might be a white cat, and so on. This semiotic process, together with the plethora of facts we can gather, will guide us to make some semblance of the above-mentioned intelligently informed decision about Columbus Day, its symbolism, and the impact the sign /Columbus/ can have.[10] All of this is part of

---

[10] Of immediate relevance here from a semiotic viewpoint is Pierre Nora's notion of "sites of memory," which he discusses

the greater research relevant to the post-enlighten-ment era we need to interrogate, which, once done, we can juxtapose to the pre-enlightenment era with regard to phenomena such as papal decrees, and con-temporary events and records that may have not been fully investigated.[11] Such intellectual activity can only add to one's ability to make the best in-formed decision possible as to one's support or lack thereof for any semblance of representational Ital-ian/American value to the sign /Columbus/.

There is already a good amount of detailed re-search on the New Orleans tragedy and the very much shredded relationship between the Italian and the U.S. governments that immediately followed

---

at length in his 1989 essay. Regarding Columbus monuments as such sites, see again Ruberto and Sciorra (64-68).

[11] In his MA thesis for CUNY's Graduate Center Liberal Studies program, Stephen J. Cerulli (2019) discusses the various dis-courses on Columbus by organizations such as the National Ital-ian American Foundation (NIAF), Order Sons and Daughters of America (OSIA), and UNICO, providing us with a cogently con-cise examination, while raising the basic question, "Whose de-cision was it for Columbus to represent Italian Americans?" The answer is not as simple as some have made it. See especially pp. 47-51. Kubal, in turn, sees the network of the lodges of the Order Sons and Daughters of America as the main network through which the *prominenti* were able to promulgate the Italian/Amer-ican Columbian myth: "Since its origins in 1905 in New York City, the OSIA has chartered more than 3,000 lodges across the United States, each promising in their constitution to sponsor an annual Columbus Day event. Many of the local lodges, along with the national OSIA office, raise funds for maintaining Co-lumbus statues" (106).

said tragedy.[12] We must be aware of those dynamics back then between the U.S. government, Italy, and the Italian/American (read, also, immigrant) population. Finally, and the basis for the first two items listed here, we must also be informed about the actions of the various Italian *prominenti* on the local, regional, and national levels.

These issues and other subject matter constitute the type of research that needs to be continually developed and hence receive requisite financial support. I underscore here *requisite* precisely because intellectual activity needs to be supported as the important societal component it is. Such intellectual work provides us with the necessary knowledge we need in order to be able to make the arguments we wish to make. Otherwise, we remain within the semiosphere of a foggy and [in]conclusive thought process.

Such research can surely be accomplished piecemeal, which is always sporadic and spans a period of time, yet it is hardly timely. Or, for the well-heeled organizations and individuals who wish to see such research performed, it can be part of a much larger system of historical and intellectual investigations that reconstruct the history and culture of Italians in the United States. This second option resembles a

---

[12] In slightly different manners and approaches, some have studied the New Orleans lynchings and the subsequent quagmire of relations between the U.S. and Italy. See, Clive Webb, Stefano Luconi, Louis Nevaer, Patrizia Salvetti, and Jennifer Barbata Jackson.

structure similar to, if not the foundation of, an Italian/American "think tank" or something similar. To date, to the chagrin of many, there is no Italian/American think tank per sé; one seems to exist for every other ethnic and/or racial group; for Italian Americans it does not.[13] The closest thing we do have to a "think tank" today is the John D. Calandra Italian American Institute, which is funded through the New York State legislature. Precisely because it is funded with tax-levied money, the Institute does not always enjoy the total freedom that a non-tax-levied institution would.[14]

The lack of such support for such an entity is one of the very fundamental reasons why there is a lack of any sort of a unified discourse on Italian Americans, however general the basis for such a discourse might need to be. Namely, what is — or, better still, what could and/or should be — that rallying point around which the greater Italian/American community might find some sense of commonality?[15] We might say that African Americans, Jewish Americans,

---

[13] For African Americans, three names that come to mind are: The Black Institute (New York). Joint Center for Political and Economic Studies (DC), The African-American Institute (DC & NY). For Jewish Americans, in turn, some names include: Jewish Institute for National Security of America (DC), Shalom Hartman Institute of North America (NY), Center for Jewish History (NY).

[14] This being the case, some complex societal issues that are more debatable than others need to be overly nuanced.

[15] I first approached this issue in 2006 and later developed it in 2010. See also Robert Viscusi's acute reasoning (2006, ix-xviii and 1-13).

and Irish Americans have that one issue, as tragic as it may be, that to some degree or another coheres the group. I have in mind, of course, slavery and its dreadful sister of outright discrimination that has resulted from it, for the first group; two millennia of *diasporic* existence and the twentieth-century, horrific holocaust, for the second group; and, for the third, the tragic, six-year potato famine of 1845 that sent over a million Irish to the United States during that time.[16]

Italian Americans have not yet decided on what the/a rallying point might be. The fact that some Italian Americans have identified Columbus and are, as an ethnic population overall, divided about him — and stridently so, at times — calls for the need for all sides to sit down and talk it out. I say all sides because, in addition to the anti- and pro-Columbus Italian Americans, there are also those who say they can go either way, and those, still, who believe that Columbus is truly irrelevant today and hence not worth the time and energy to expend.

Indeed, I contend that Italian Americans should be very much concerned with the various ways in which social issues continue to impact our popula-

---

[16] There are, to be sure, many positive aspects about each of these cultures that clearly contribute to each group's coherence. However, we surely do not err in seeing these more tragic events as the more cohesive element. Further still, while I would generally eschew such inter-ethnic comparisons, sometimes we need to engage in such intellectual activity in order to make our point, as this is a constant refrain with many members of an Italian/American in-group. Thus, in so doing, we *speak their language*.

tion at large: and here, I have in mind notions of class and whiteness. This second aspect, especially, brings us inevitably to that slippery slope of (a) how exactly do we define whiteness and/or (b) the desire to be white. Being of southern European origins, we know that historically Italian Americans have not always been considered white, and as a result, those of the great Italian emigration who hailed from below the "Linea Spezia" were in fact placed into a non-white category for a period of time. Hence, our obligation to negotiate said slippery slope seems thus inevitable; it is an obligation, I would underscore, for both the scholar and the — sometimes self-appointed — community leader. Said obligation calls for some form and/or manner of amalgamation of both sectors of Italian America. Unfortunately, the conjunction of the academy and society at large is woefully lacking among Italian Americans. This has come to the fore more recently during the fall 2017 campaign to save Columbus Day. Some recently organized groups, Columbus Heritage Coalition and Save Columbus Day, to mention two, have all but eschewed any input from the academy. Indeed, a few members of these and other groups, in their vigor to cancel out any possible discussion and/or collaboration between the two communities, have, what can readily assume to be purposefully, obfuscated positions of neutrality taken by some Italian/American organizations, as I demonstrated in my column in *La Voce di New York*, "The Columbus Controversy and the Politics of Omission" (2017c); they have defined said neutrality within the superficial thought process of "with us or against us" only. A fundamental book regarding Italian Americans and whiteness is the collection edited by Jennifer Guglielmo and Salvatore Salerno, *Are Italians White?*[17]

2. ACKNOWLEDGE THAT FOR ITALIAN AMERICANS Columbus is a symbol of *courage, perseverance,* and *exploration*, qualities that resonate with the history of the Italian immigration experience to the U.S. Acknowledge also — once the research is completed and the argument articulated — that while he and/or his crew may have committed acts of imprisonment or violence, said acts are to be condemned. That while "indentured servitude" was a consequence of war at the time, the Slave Trade industry to bring over Africans began in 1619 in this hemisphere.

It is an absolute necessity to acknowledge the negative legacy of the discovery of the Americas. Through careful research, it might indeed be argued that they are the unfortunate consequences *that followed,* and *not* the *desired intentions* of, Columbus in making his voyage. I realize that here I am approaching that quagmire of "intentionality." In order to avoid having to engage in a concerted discussion of its philosophical

---

[17] See, also, my essay, "The Semiotics of Labeling" (2020b).

underpinnings, I will state here that I am presuming we could arrive at some semblance of an answer — however fleeting it may seem — if we engaged in the examination of the documentation available to us. To be sure, short of anything Columbus himself might have written, we can only depend on what is available to us and expend our time and effort on such historical realia. To this point, in the debatable document, *The First Voyage*, we read the following:

> They [Natives] should be good *servants* and intelligent, for I observed that they quickly took in what was said to them, and I believe that they would easily be made Christians, as it appeared to me that they had no religion. I, our Lord being pleased, will take hence, at the time of my departure, six natives for your Highnesses, that they may learn to speak. (38; emphasis mine)

I referenced the text as debatable for the very reason that it contains, as Felipe Fernández-Armesto states, "inevitable corruptions introduced into a text avowedly based on a copy" (1991, 68). He also underscores the presence of "four distinct voices that are hard to distinguish from the rest of the text (168):

> There are parenthetical or marginal comments inserted by Las Casas ... which are usually marked by their sententious tone: the editor marvels, for instance, at his hero's insensitivity to the evils of slavery, or praises his unshakable faith in God.

There are passages of paraphrase in which Las Casas narrates the events without disclosing the relationship of his own text to the original... (1991, 68)

Fernández-Armesto continues to underscore other issues that call into question not only the text's voice, but, in addition, what the intentionality of said text might be. Namely, who is speaking, and what are we to take away from such a text? This is especially true since such polyvocality of the text is further compounded by a "prolific direct quotation ... about the Indians ... unquestionably selected to reflect the editor's [Las Casas] priorities rather than the author's [Columbus] and confirms ... Las Casas's image of the Indians as uncorrupted, peaceful inhabitants of a world of sylvan innocence" (1991, 68). Hence, questions arise if only on a textual level, which, once more, calls into question how much the reader can depend on the text's representative quality — read, *authority* — and currency of its presumed author.

In addition to what Fernández-Armesto underscores about the ambiguous voice of Columbus's *The First Voyage*, a second text to interrogate is by Francisco de Bobadilla's inquiry into Columbus, which he compiled in 1500. The report finally came to light in 2006, when it was discovered and then published by Consuelo Varela and Isabel Aguirre in a book entitled *La caída e Cristóbal Colón. El juicio de Bobadilla*, which contains Bobadilla's "Pesquisa" (inquiry). Some want to see the document as a false, if not at the very least highly defective, report. Raphael Ortiz writes: "The Bobadilla report is full of half-truths, innuendos, double-talking, slanders, lies, etc. As for Consuelo's book, I will give it a three-star rating just because the transcription of the document carries great historical interest" (2021). If such a document is "full of half-truths, innuendos, double-talking, and the book itself "carries great historical interest," then should one not interrogate further such a finding? Ortiz does not.[18] Others, instead, see it differently. In reviewing a book by Angel Rodriguez Alvarez,[19] Miguel Sague sees *La caída* as an important source in confirming that "the real person who really established the pattern of cruel and inhuman treatment of the Taino that eventually became the norm throughout all of Spanish America was none other than Christopher Columbus himself. He placed the most stubborn obstacles to allowing the Tainos to acquire the status that would free them from the abuse. That status was Christian conversion. He did it consciously and on purpose so that he could exploit them more effectively" (2008). Either way, a

---

[18] Carol Delany, in turn, seems to deal with Bobadilla's report on through secondary and tertiary channels. Indeed, were one to defend Columbus, one might want to rely on more secure acts of referentiality. She actually references the Bobadilla text only once.

[19] Sague's review is of Angel Rodriguez Alvarez's *Mitologia Taina o Eyeri Ramon Pane y La Relacion Sobre LasAntiguedades de los Indios*.

strong sense of intellectualism would warrant further investigation by both sides.

Moving to yet another text, one might surely bring into the discussion the Doctrine of Discovery that was, as one is wont to say with such vast time lapses, the practice of the time. On the other hand, here, as in other similar cases, one runs the risk of having to deal with the issue of evaluating behavior of yesteryear — however far in the past said behavior may have taken place — through a moral and ethical lens of today. Thus, at this juncture, it becomes a question of one decision against another; there is no one unmitigated choice by which we evaluate, today, the events of centuries ago. That said, if we are apt to remedy, for example, slavery in the U.S. in some form or another, Columbus, too, one might say, must be evaluated accordingly. This is one of the conundrums that both defenders and detractors of Columbus must confront. Further still, in like fashion, one must not ignore the genocide and other tragedies that befell Native Americans.

In so doing, then, one points to the inevitable negative phenomena that were a part of what was, in turn, a major geographical and philosophical paradigm shift within Western Civilization. Some have called it the major act of the millennium, the unification of two worlds, superseding to a remarkable degree both the Renaissance and the Age of Enlightenment. Neil deGrasse Tyson, in turn, goes one step further; he called Columbus's voyage the "single most important event in the history of the human species" in that Columbus "reconnect[ed] the human species that ha[d] been separated for 10,000 years" (Rose). William Connell, in turn, speaks to the importance of agriculture as Columbus's legacy: "[I]f all the remaining monuments to him were to be destroyed, Columbus would still be with us. And the reason is straightforward: October 12, 1492 was the most important date in human history, at least since the invention of agriculture. From that date the world that we now live in had its beginning" (2020).[20]

What both deGrasse Tyson and Connell do in making such a statement is to think beyond "the immediate consequences and look at his broader, unintended impacted [sic] on the human species as a whole" (Rose). By considering Columbus's feat of his transatlantic voyage and not the navigator himself as individual and all that it pertains, places him more within the realm of the representational. Thus, as either great sailor or precursor to turn-of-the-century immigration, Columbus must then be presented *not* as an individual, rather as a *symbol* of courage, perseverance, and exploration, all those qualities that intimately and integrally resonate with the *everyman*, as we are wont to say; the "povero cristo," as one might

---

[20] Anthony C. Wisniewski articulates a similar notion in his Op. Ed for the *Ames Tribune*: "Whatever his personal faults, without Columbus, there would be no United States, one of the relatively few countries in the world that guarantees the rights of individuals to petition their government peacefully through demonstrations."

say in Italian, those afflicted and destitute Italians, especially at the turn of the twentieth century, who had to leave Italy in order to survive. Hence, their *courage* to leave, their requisite *perseverance* in order to survive and overcome the then anti-Italian discrimination, all of which is accompanied by their essential over-riding spirit of *exploration*.

While pro-Columbus Italian Americans might make an argument similar to what I have just outlined above, there is one aspect of their reasoning that surely puts them back on their heels. I believe it is imperative that what Italian Americans who defend Columbus *cannot* do is characterize the anti-Columbus movement as an anti-Italian movement, claiming that attacks on Columbus statues are intentional and purposeful attacks on the "civil rights" of Italian Americans. It is a one-dimensional and sketchy extrapolation with no indices of fact. There is no credible evidence that the desire to take down statues of Columbus or protest against Columbus Day is anti-Italian. On the contrary, in Bennie Klain's short documentary, *Columbus Day Legacy*, the late Native American, militant activist Russel Means clearly declared his support of Italian/American celebrations of culture. In *Columbus Day Legacy*, he states the following to his Italian/American interlocutors during a radio program: "We've always advocated an Italian pride day" (Klain, 5:24); he then continued later in the program: "Why don't they talk about Galileo, Leonardo da Vinci, Joe DiMaggio, Frank Sinatra, all the icons of the

Italian race? [...] All we ask is to change the name" (Klain, 21:57-20:20). His words — "We've always advocated an Italian pride day" and "All we ask is to change the name" — need to be underscored precisely because he is, *de facto*, supporting the celebration of Italian heritage while decrying the label — "Columbus Day" — affixed to it.

Such support by Native Americans on behalf of Italian/American heritage is articulated by Mike L. Graham in a letter to the Order Sons of Italy in America.[21] According to the website where Graham's letter to OSIA appears, "OSIA wanted to know what it would take for Indians to stop protesting their national holiday under the name of Columbus Day." In his response to OSIA Graham concluded:

> The Native American community *stands ready to join side by side with all Italian Americans in the celebration of their heritage under any name other than Columbus.* The Native American community *fully respects all Italians, but will not show support for Columbus, the man,* nor support his having a national holiday in America. (emphasis added)

We see in these two instances — one with Means, the other with Graham — that an unmitigated support of Italian heritage and of any and all celebrations by Native Americans is conditioned by one factor only,

---

[21] Graham's signature appears with the title "member Oklahoma Cherokee Nation, Founder United Native America.

that there be no mention nor celebration of Christopher Columbus.

In like fashion, Kubal underscored this lack of anti-Italianism in his description of the agreement made for the re-instatement of the Columbus Day parade in Denver in 2000. It was dependent on a four-part accord between the city of Denver, the D-AIM (Denver American Indian Movement), Italian American leaders, and other community leaders (124). Kubal wrote:

> The agreement said that D-AIM would promise to call off the protest and *help the Italians celebrate an Italian heritage parade* if the Italian activists would agree to *not mention the name or present the likeness of Columbus* in any part of the parade or other ceremonies. They also had to agree to *not hold ceremonies around the Columbus statue in downtown Denver* and to *forbid all participants from using the words or symbols of Columbus.* (124; emphasis added)

At first glance, one might suggest excessive prohibition to the presence of anything that conjures up the sign /Columbus/. But that is not my point here. Instead, what was of ultimate significance in 2000, as it will prove to be eleven years later, in 2011, in the very same city and with the same D-AIM and Italian/American leaders in Klain's *Columbus Day Legacy*, is that there was no discussion *against* celebrat-

ing Italian heritage. On the contrary, we see, in fact,
that the D-AIM was ready to help the Italians celebrate an Italian heritage parade, given the adherence
to other provisos of the agreement with regard to an
embargo of any semblance of any form of verbal or
visual representation of Columbus. Thus, given the
indices of fact in this regard, to claim anti-Italian discrimination, precisely because it is *not* embedded as
an intention into the anti-Columbus movement — as
both the 2000 D-AIM and the late Russell Means
demonstrated in 2000 and 2011, respectively — can
only prove to be a major distraction and, hence, bring
unnecessary criticism to the pro-Columbus movement. In so doing, the pro-Columbus advocates themselves create an unwarranted critique from the anti-
Columbus movement that can only set them back on
their heels precisely because adherence to a false in-
dex, such as anti-Columbus protests equate to anti-
Italianism, plants willy-nilly semiotic doubt in other
indices that might otherwise have ample value.

There is, moreover, an unintended consequence
to any unsubstantiated claim of anti-Italian discrimination, which, I would contend, is amplified in this
situation. As many would agree, there still exists a
practice of activities and comments that constitute a
series of microaggressions toward Italian Americans
in society today. That subtle form of prejudice that is
often unintentional may raise its ugly head in the
guise of an off-handed comment ("Judge [fill in the
blank with an *Italian/American* name] is so articulate

and fair in decision making!" said with a tone of surprise), an uncalculatedly painful joke ("Oh, you're Italian! Are you connected?"), or the so-called cute and/or funny advertisement, such as Eataly's truffle commercial ("Take home an Italian [truffle], it's worth the smell!"). I have documented other examples in various blogs over the years.[22] In some cases, the aggression is surely "micro-"; yet, in other cases, the aggression is more blatant and, hence, "macro-." A response of indignity and umbrage on the part of an Italian American today is often met with incredulity on the part of the non-Italian American, with a reaction such as, "Really?" You're offended?" or "Don't be so sensitive!" If we then cry anti-Italian discrimination where it does not exist, as in the case of the anti-Columbus movement, how then might we expect those very real and truly harmful micro- if not macroaggressions to be recognized as such, with the requisite gravity and earnestness that would necessitate an eventual sensitization and consequential change in thinking on the perpetrator's part?

In this regard, Anne Paolucci saw the entire enterprise of anti-Italian discrimination of any sort as "misplaced fervor" (15). With reference to Columbus, she stated:

---

[22] With regard to some of my blogs, one need only access i-Italy.org (2016, 2014, 2013a-d, 2012a-b, 2011, 2010, 2009, 2008, and subsequent articles in *La voce di New York* (2020, 2018, 2017a-c, 2016).

> This misplaced fervor was starkly evident during
> the Quincentenary, when Italian-Americans ac-
> cused those who were "bashing" Columbus of
> "discrimination." Against whom? Columbus was
> more Portuguese than Italian; but aside from that
> and more to the point: was "discrimination" the
> only reply indignant Italian-Americans could
> muster in response to accusations that could only
> be properly dismissed by accepting certain grim
> facts and answering them knowledgeably? (15)

Her last sentence in this paragraph is, for sure, most
poignant. It is a question of being informed as best
possible, of having at one's fingertips those bits and
pieces of historical facts that can aid one in his/her
argument, not to mention the more basic awareness
of historical moments that are sometimes absent.
The result of such ignorance, according to Paolucci
is that "arguments, if offered, were often flimsy or
outright misleading" (16). "Infinitely more effec-
tive," she continues, "would have been events and
projects that presented Columbus in perspective,
not disclaiming but, rather, explaining certain facts
by placing them in their proper historical context"
(16). It is the concept of "in perspective" that undergirds Paolucci's argument here; we simply cannot
ignore history, as she continues:

> The facts of history cannot be changed or rewritten
> to accord with today's "politically correct" views
> or with priorities not current in Columbus's time.

But by the same token, the facts cannot be ignored to avoid certain realities. The history of conquest is the history of the world since time began (at least as far back as records exist). Unpleasant deeds committed to secure power through conquest is part of history — an ugly truth. [...] It is the realistic premise on which history finally comes to rest. (16)

While she is pro-Columbus as we understand by her first sentence, historical facts nonetheless are fundamental to her general thinking: "Unpleasant deeds committed to secure power through conquest is part of history — an ugly truth."[23] Any answers to counter the anti-Columbus movement must be "just as astute and discriminating" (16).

---

[23] Paolucci discusses further the misplaced defensiveness of anti-Italian discrimination. She continues in her essay: "For other reasons, 'discrimination' carries little weight when leveled against the producers of such profitable television series as *The Sopranos* (with a large audience) or such films as *The Godfather* — a genial account, among other things, of the power assumed by a few strong men to protect themselves and their community in the early days, when Italians had to deal with a hostile environment and had to turn to their own, for justice. ... {A]re we pressing the wrong buttons? Do we really expect Hollywood to apologize for *The Godfather*? Why should it? The film has become a classic and with good reason: it's one of the best ever made, with a superb cast; a realistic account of the hostility between the Irish and the Italians, in the early days; a drama of power as it takes on the law, and of gradual changes that came about within the 'families' at that time. In the end, of course, all arguments disappear: it's only fiction ... but also a piece of history" (16-17).

Finally, in this regard, the Columbus statue *qua* the sign /Columbus/ would need to be reclassified in today's general climate of "hate statues." After the Charlottesville tragedy of 2017, Melissa Mark-Viverito, then Speaker the City Council of New York, demanded that the City examine its "hate statues," and within that group she clumped the Columbus monument at Columbus Circle in mid-town Manhattan. In demanding the removal of the J. Marion Sims statue, she rightfully stated:

> At a time when Neo-Nazis, white nationalists and hateful right wing [sic] extremists run rampant throughout the country with impunity, we must send a definitive message that the despicable acts of J. Marion Sims are repugnant and reprehensible. J. Marion Sims conducted horrific, painful, medical atrocities on non-anesthetized enslaved Black women with free-reign. Mayor de Blasio and the Parks Department must remove this repugnant statue from our neighborhood once and for all. (Anonymous)

The intentionality of the likes of Sims (his torturous medical experiments on "non-anesthetized enslaved Black women"), the *raison d'être* of the Confederate States of America (a treasonous breakaway from the U.S.A.), and the theory of white supremacy that undergirds Neo-Nazis, white nationalists, and hateful right-wingers (anti-Semitic, racist, genocidal), all of which we witness to our chagrin today, are surely things to eschew and condemn.

The question begged here is thus the following: Should we include in this group the likes of Christopher Columbus, whose original intentionality, one might try to argue, included none of the above despicable behavior we ascribe to the groups listed by Speaker Mark-Viverito? Columbus's primary motives, one might further contend at first glance, had no seemingly intentional, disreputable and/or loathsome aims. That said, then, back in 2017, those in defense of Columbus should have acted accordingly in reaction to Speaker Mark-Viverito; they should have immediately uncoupled the Columbus statue from the other statues of more recent referentiality through a process of systematic reasoning, beginning from what we might know, if not more likely assume, to have been his intentions and chronology. It may not be too late to do so now; one might indeed take up such argumentation and uncouple Columbus even now, as one moves forward.[24] After all, Columbus is from one half of a millennium ago, so, to put it succinctly, one has the time. But here, as in other cases of a similar nature, the competence and articulation of the professionally trained scholar of history are of the

---

[24] I refer to Wisniewski's above-cited Op. Ed. for a similar thought: "Somehow in the storyline, Columbus and Confederate statues have been wrongly blended as co-equal symbols of a racist past as the nation grapples with the killing of George Floyd, an African American man, by a white Minneapolis police officer."

utmost importance. As we shall see later, some wish to identify Columbus with major human accomplishments only, downplaying, at best, atrocities that were both contemporary and subsequent.

Further still, yet not wanting to exonerate Columbus of all of his behavior, one might want to distinguish the chronology involved, that the phenomenology of Columbus's era is pre-Enlightenment, whereas the phenomena of someone like a J. Marion Sims, the Neo-Nazis, the white nationalists, and other hateful right-wing extremists — as well as the Confederate States of America — are post-Enlightenment and therefore imbued with a different value system that, in both theory and practice, have at their base a rationale of societal interaction and exchange that is different from that value system of the end of the 15th century. If anything, one might indeed decide to reposition Columbus historically and place him alongside the likes of George Washington and Thomas Jefferson, two other remarkedly flawed individuals (i.e., owners of slaves) according to a post-Enlightenment / post-Civil Rights reflection and judgement, yet whose accomplishments in the end save them from total banishment from history.

In like fashion, then, one might try to save Columbus while acknowledging his flaws of the time. Once again, as with the first above-listed accomplishment, any research for this task is time consuming and complex, and it should be executed by a professional scholar, if not a team of qualified scholars:

This is not a job for the amateur. To date, much has been written and much has been debated, and not always by the historically trained and adequately informed; as it stands, there are simply too many facile and anecdotal attempts at defending Columbus. Much more has to be done by the professionally trained and accomplished scholar. Whether one is pro- or anti-Columbus, research on the navigator must include at its base, first and foremost, ample examination of those documents that might shed greater light on late fifteenth- and early sixteenth-century thought processes. This has yet to take place within the context of Italian Americans and their entanglement with the Columbus Affair. Connell attempts as much in his article (2013). But it is an article in a journal, an excellent introduction to the issues at hand, which, some might agree, sees the Columbus Day as "an event, not a person" (145). The parsing of the pertinent texts of that era and of those equally relevant texts and events of the 1892 celebration need to be reconciled with the "actions and attitudes that were typical of" (145) the fifteen century and against the decision today to re-visit our history and re-consider its relationship to present-day thinking. It may be asking for a great deal, indeed too much. That notwithstanding, we can point to one of the more complete works to date, especially within an inter-ethnic framework, I would submit at this juncture, that is Kubal's book (2009). Stephen Cerulli, in turn, contextualizes the studies by Kubal and Ruberto and Sciorra, demonstrating a congruent vision by both an external (Kubal) and an internal (Ruberto and Sciorra) voice.

Felipe Fernández-Armesto underscores the dangers of writing on that about which one may know very little, if anything at all, and, as well, within the framework of a discipline in which you have not been professionally trained.[26] In his 2011 review of four books on Columbus,[27] Fernández-Armesto tells us that to "write well about history you do not need a Ph.D., just a few rare but accessible qualities: insatiable curiosity, critical intellect, *disciplined* imagination, *indefatigability in the pursuit of truth* and a slightly weird vocation for trying to get to know dead people by studying the sources they have left us" (emphasis added). But Fernández-Armesto, the staunch historian that he is, also tells us in a more serious pose that it is imperative that the scholar command "[competence] in research," possess a healthy dose of "critical discrimination," and, as well, retain a sense of humility throughout the discovery of facts and his/her construction of a "rational chronology" and "coherent narrative." This is not an easy enterprise, as Hayden White explains:

---

[26] Fernández-Armesto, is, for all practical purposes, our living expert on Columbus and other themes of historical navigation, having authored at least four of his close to two dozen books in this regard (1991, 2007, 2010a, 2010b).

[27] The four books are by Lawrence Bergreen (2011), Nigel Cliff (2012), Carol Delaney (2011), and Douglas Hunter (2011).

[I]n his efforts to reconstruct "what happened" in any given period of history, the historian inevitably must include in his narrative an account of some event or complex of events for which the facts that would permit a plausible explanation of its occurrence are lacking. And this means that the historian must "interpret" his materials by filling in the gaps in his information on inferential or speculative grounds. A historical narrative is thus necessarily a mixture of adequately and inadequately explained events, a congeries of established and inferred facts, at once a representation that is an interpretation and an interpretation that passes for an explanation of the whole process mirrored in the narrative. (281)

This is the task of the historian *in nuce*. The risks, in turn, are high, as Fernández-Armesto tells us in his review:

[S]cholars may have encouraged these amateurs' imprudence by publishing English translations of many of the sources. *Translated sources attract errors just as translated scriptures foment heresies*, and when the inexperienced attempt their own translations, the results can be even worse. Mr. Bergreen, Mr. Cliff, Mr. Hunter and Ms. Delaney *do not have the linguistic skills to master the literature on their own*. They all seem to be *illiterate in Latin* and *imperfectly assured* in handling the sources in Romance languages. (2011; emphasis added)

I have made this digression about the historian's task and responsibilities because of the dangers such errors in narrative chronology and misinterpretations, due to poor or inexistent language skills, can extract. The purist some may accuse him of being, Fernández-Armesto prefers an adequate knowledge of Latin, French, and Spanish in order to construct a "rational chronology" and "coherent narrative," as I cited above. These are, in the end, basic tools the historian must possess in her/his arsenal; they allow the historian to access certain knowledge that otherwise s/he would not discover. Such a preparation allows for a less difficult task for the necessary filling "in the gaps," as Hayden White reminds us above.

It is thus through a thorough exploration of various realia — consulting those old books in depositories no longer on the shelves, shifting through those archives that require limited access, processing other material old and new in other languages — that we can construct the "rational chronology" and "coherent narrative" that Fernández-Armesto underscores as the lynchpins for accurate and hence adequate history. In this regard, therefore, as I highlight one example, we might better understand the issue of prisoners vs. slaves within the Columbian semiosphere by interrogating, in addition to other issues, two documents of discovery; the first, a papal decree issued by Pope Nicholas V in 1452 that sanctioned and promoted conquest, colonization, and exploitation of non-Christian territories and the peoples who inhabited said lands. At one point in this Papal Bull, we read:

> "... invadendi, conquirendi, expugnandi et sub-jugandi, illorumque personas *in perpetuam servi-tutem redigendi...*" (24; emphasis added)[28]

This brief example highlights Fernández-Armesto's insistence on the scholar's adequate preparation in the intellectual handling of historical facts and events. First, there is the very fact that this Papal Bull actually exists and, as such, disenfranchises to the point of dehumanization the inhabitants of lands discovered by European Catholics. Second, these very few words in the original debunk in its entirety any validity to the distinction between slaves and prisoners. A "slave" in Latin is "servus," of the same etymological family of *servitutem,* whereas a "prisoner" is "captivus," of the same family of "captivitatem." Were we indeed dealing with prisoners instead of slaves, then the 1452 Papal Bull might read, "in ... *captivitatem* redigendi" and not "in ... *servitutem* redigendi," the former implicitly signaling some endpoint of captivity, the latter not necessarily so, which indeed here is underscored by the adjective "perpetuam."[29]

---

[28] "... invade, conquer, storm, and subjugate their people by reducing them into lifelong enslavement ..." (my translation).
[29] Fernández-Armesto deals with the issue of slavery in his examination of Columbus (1991, 68, 142, *passim*).

This 1452 doctrine of discovery was upheld by Pope Alexander VI on May 4, 1493, which supported Spain's exclusive rights to the territory discovered by Columbus the previous year.[30] These are significant if only because it gives us both a more direct line to and confirmation of the thinking process of the era. One might indeed argue that thus began the conquest and colonization of the New World and, eventually, the spread up into North America. The obvious question, of course, is how this impacts our thoughts today on Columbus. Is there a straight line from Columbus and his deeds to the eventual appropriation of lands owned by Native Americans? Well, the answer, one might say as we read below, is, yes. In a controversy over title of land in the early 1800s, the U. S. Supreme Court decided that Native American tribes did not have the absolute right to cede title of land. In the case, Johnson vs. McIntosh (1823), the U. S. Supreme Court decided:

> Not only has the practice of all civilized nations been in conformity with this doctrine, but the

---

[30] We read that the 1493 decree "established a demarcation line one hundred leagues west of the Azores and Cape Verde Islands and assigned Spain the exclusive right to acquire territorial possessions and to trade in all lands west of that line. All others were forbidden to approach the lands west of the line without special license from the rulers of Spain. This effectively gave Spain a monopoly on the lands in the New World." See the original document with translation on the website of The Gilder Lehrman Institute of American History (www. gilderlehrman.org).

whole theory of their titles to lands in America, rests upon the hypothesis, *that the Indians had no right of soil as sovereign, independent states. Discovery is the foundation of title, in European nations, and this overlooks all proprietary rights in the natives.* The sovereignty and eminent domain thus acquired, *necessarily precludes the idea of any other sovereignty existing within the same limits.* The subjects of the discovering nation must necessarily be bound by the declared sense of their own government, as to the extent of this sovereignty, and the domain acquired with it. Even if it should be admitted that the Indians were originally an independent people, they have ceased to be so. *A nation that has passed under the dominion of another, is no longer a sovereign state.* (567-568; emphasis added)[32]

Why is such a case so important, especially more than three hundred years later? It demonstrates how the Columbus phenomenon and its subsequent consequences in the form of Pope Alexander VI's "Demarcation Bull" led to the cancellation of Native/American nations as sovereign states.[33] No small deed, to be

---

[32] As a side note, "Chief Justice John Marshall (1755-1835) had large real estate holdings (as did his family and friends) that would have been affected if the case had been decided contrary to those interests. Rather than remove himself from the case, however, the Chief Justice wrote the decision for a unanimous United States Supreme Court" (Frichner, 11).

[33] I have opted for "nation" and not tribes, bands, pueblos, communities, or native villages, among others.

sure. The rest, as we say, is history, which under-scores why, today, Native Americans readily trace back their current challenges to 1492 and those sub-sequent acts of genocide and other tragedies that con-tinued to — what we might consider the major tragic marker for Native Americans — Wounded Knee in 1890, and afterward up through to 2013.[34] During the period from 2007 to 2013, for example, a number of resolutions were adopted that finally "asserted Na-tive rights" (*Doctrine of Discover: A Timeline*).

Such a tragedy, among others, surely explains why Native Americans even today would consider the Columbian legacy a most negative one, regardless of the positive aspect that others see in Columbus's voyages. I would recall at this point Neil deGrasse Tyson's above-cited characterization Columbus's crossing the Atlantic as the "single most important event in the history of the human species." This is, of course, the conundrum. What do we do with some-one like Columbus who, as history would seem to have it, spans the moral spectrum of behavior from good to evil? From "reconnect[ing] the human spe-cies that ha[d] been separated for 10,000 years," deGrasse Tyson stated, to opening up the New World to the victimization of the Doctrine of Discovery, as

---

[34] I highlight here Wounded Knee because it was Dee Brown's best-selling book, *Buried My Heart at Wounded Knee*, that raised awareness on a more general scale of the 1890 tragedy. The title, I would mention, comes Stephen Vincent Bennet's 1931 poem, "American names."

others would surmise, Columbus remains in that category of the flawed individual who accomplished the
unexpected. As stated above, he might be coupled to
Washington and Jefferson, two other flawed individuals according to a post-Enlightenment / post-Civil
Rights reflection and judgement, whose accomplishments in the end, so it seems, save them from total
banishment from history. This is the philosophical
enigma that begs our attention.

It is, I would contend, a question of moral relativism and semiotics. For moral relativism, the question
is: What are those historical phenomena and how far
do we go back into history and judge said phenomena and/or individuals, and do we engage them with
or without prejudice? Or, one might add colloquially,
Where is the line in the sand, if any? All of this is dependent on our own cultural reservoir and what we
bring to the interpretive table. Yes, it is a question of
interpretation, as Hayden White wrote back in 1973:
"The historian has to interpret his materials in order
to construct the moving pattern of images in which
the form of the historical process is to be mirrored"
(282). That said, mine is not a rhetorical exercise, it is
not a syntactical, lexical, and/or semantic desired act
of prestidigitation, precisely because this is what lies
at the base of our philosophical conundrum. If we are
not in favor of Columbus, what do we do, then, with
others such as, Washington and Jefferson? If we are
in favor of Columbus, what do we do with those
other figures and/or symbols that are problematic?

For example, how do we reconcile something like the Balbo Monument in Chicago, a 2,000-year-old column taken from Porta Marina, Ostia, outside of Rome, and gifted to Chicago by Italy's Fascist government and delivered most ceremoniously by Fascist aviator Italo Balbo?[35] Or, more recently in the news, there is movement afoot to remove a Columbus statue in Brooklyn sculpted by Emma Stebbins (Duggan). Best known for her stature, "Angel of the Waters" (1873), located in New York's Central Park, Stebbins was the first woman to receive a major sculptural commission.[36] Further still, she was gay and lived openly with the actress Charlotte Cushman "in Rome for twelve years, until Cushman learned she had breast cancer. They returned to the United States in 1870, abandoning several of Stebbins's unfinished pieces in Italy" (Harlan).

At this juncture, I return to the idea that for Columbus to survive, albeit with ample scars, one may

[35] Italo Balbo (June 6, 1896 –June 28, 1940) was a member of the *Camicie Nere*; he was Italy's Marshal of the Air Force; as well, the Governor General of Lybia; and, also, the Commander-in-Chief of Italian North Africa, all of which had tragic consequences. Had he lived and had the Fascist Regime survived, he might have very well followed Benito Mussolini as head of the Regime.

[36] As we read in Jennifer Harlan's *New York Times* obituary, "the angel has been visitant in movies like 'Enchanted' and 'Elf' and in television shows like 'Sex and the City.' Perhaps most famously, the fountain served as the setting for the final scene of Tony Kushner's theatrical masterpiece about AIDS and homophobia during the Reagan era, 'Angels in America.' (And it features in the opening credits of the HBO mini-series version of "Angels," hauntingly lifting her head toward the viewer.)."

surely recognize his crossing as the "most important event in ... history," as deGrasse Tyson states, but one must then rise above the literal and enter into the realm of the symbolic, as I mentioned earlier in this essay. Otherwise, /Columbus/ or Columbus has not a snowball's chance in Hades in surviving. The afore-mentioned tryptic of courage, perseverance, and exploration that one can readily ascribe to Columbus, can be equally valuable in describing those qualities that the poor Italian immigrant had to muster up in order to leave his/her small country village, to travel to Palermo, Naples, or Genova, and to board the vessel that would be his/her domicile for thirty subsequent days in steerage.

3. EMPHASIZE THE CONTRIBUTIONS OF IMMIGRANT ANCESTORS and current Italian Americans to all levels of U.S. society — local, state, national — in government, labor, education, the arts (literature, film, painting, other visual media), the social sciences, business, and other sectors of society.

Scholars of Italian/American studies bump up against a wall of frustration when those who are in positions of influence — especially those who are the self-appointed and inexperienced in certain facets of Italian Americana — exhibit little to no specific knowledge of (1) the trials and tribulations first met by the immigrants and their progeny, and (2) the very significant contributions both Italian immigrants and their progeny have made to the U.S.[37] Hence, it is especially incumbent on these self-appointed individuals to possess an integral reservoir of knowledge about Italian Americans. Or, they should be willing to enlist the assistance of the expert intellectuals — read, professionally trained scholars — on the subject matter at hand. Surely, as Italian Americans we can readily celebrate the likes of Dante, Machiavelli, Leonardo, Michelangelo, and other Italians who have made indelible marks throughout. And why not? They are, after all, the major figures of Italy's history and culture. But they are just that, Italians, *not* Italian Americans, and hence they do not constitute the bulk of the foundation of our Italian/American talking points. Indeed, this is also a point in defense of relegating Columbus to the category of Italians and *not* Italian Americans. It recalls, that is, the late Russell Means's exhortation that Italian Americans celebrate more Italian Americans and not Italians. Or, at the very least, not compromised Italians.

Our Italian/American talking points, on the other hand, must include, among many more, the likes of the following: Fiorello LaGuardia, Mario Cuomo, and Geraldine Ferraro among elected officials; Luigi An-

---

[37] Regarding a history of immigration to the United States from a more pluralistic perspective, I refer the reader to Robert L. Fleegler's *Ellis Island Nation* and his analysis of contributionism, "the idea that newcomers strengthened the American economy and culture while also accepting certain American norms" (191).

tonini, Carlo Tresca, and Angela Bambace among activists and unionists; Angelo Patri and Leonard Co-
vello among educators; Don DeLillo, Lisa Scottoline,
Adriana Trigiani, and Diane di Prima among writers;
Francis Ford Coppola, Martin Scorsese, and Nancy
Savoca among filmmakers; Joseph Stella, Frank Stella,
Ralph Fasanella, Vito Acconci, and Bill Viola among
painters and other visual artists; and so on. We all
need to include, to be sure, but we also need to go beyond the likes of Frank Sinatra, Joe DiMaggio, and
Dean Martin. We need to add to this popular trio.
And, in the end, we need to be amply informed on
how Italian immigrants and their progeny have had
and continue to have an impact on the United States.

As a scholar and — may I add — cultural broker
as Dean of the John D. Calandra Italian American Institute and co-publisher, I remain firmly resolute
that such an inventory of knowledge is a *sine qua non*
for anyone who steps out front as a presumed leader
of any valid and credible association that is dedicated to the history and culture of Italians in the
United States. Italian Americans simply cannot af-
ford to be caught off guard, if not exposed as uninformed, about the history of Native Americans if one
so desires to maintain that Columbus remain a representational figure for Italian Americans; *representational* precisely because it is through the symbolic, I
am convinced, that /Columbus/ as sign might survive.

While it is improbable to ascertain his opinion of Columbus as symbol for Italian Americans, one Italian American who has championed the Native American is the actor, Michael Dante.[39] Among his 30 films and 150 TV appearances, Dante played three roles as a Native American: Red Hawk (*Apache Rifles*, 1964), Crazy Horse (*The Legend of Custer*, 1967), and Winterhawk (*Winterhawk*, 1975). It was his title role in the 1975 film, *Winterhawk* that triggered in him a passion and interest in Native Americans. The film's story is about an "Indian chief" from the Blackfoot tribe, whose attempts to get help for his people infected by smallpox, is betrayed by the very people from whom he sought help (the White people); his reaction was to resort to desperate measures in order to obtain the vaccine that would ultimately save his tribe. *Winterhawk* became Dante's main cinematic challenge. Once the film's director, Charles B. Pierce, rejected the idea of a sequel, Dante bought the rights with the hopes of securing funding for a second film. Throughout these efforts Dante eventually scripted a second screenplay which now appears as a novella, *Winterhawk's Land*.

[39] Born Ralph Vitti in Stamford, CT, he was at first a professional baseball player for the Boston Braves and then the Washington Senators. Soon thereafter, discovered by band leader Tommy Dorsey, Dante began an acting career that continued through to the late 1980s, with an occasional appearance thereafter. Most recently, he has authored three books. For more on Michael Dante, see www.michaeldanteway.com.

Dante's recognition of the perils of Native Americans throughout nineteen-century U.S. history, especially, is what stands out here. Through his written sequel to the film *Winterhawk* and his 2017 interview with Ed Robertson on TV Confidential, Dante is adamant that the U.S., and especially the younger generations, are knowledgeable about the "perils" that Native Americans faced, "hunger, disease and the railroad, possibly creating a genocide," as he stated to Robertson (Robertson, 36:00) in 2017.[40] He underscored how unscrupulous railroad magnates and the military were bent on taking what they needed (10 miles on each side of the tracks) in constructing the railroad. Indeed, Dante continues in his conversation to bemoan our collective lack of history, not realizing that the "blazing of the West, [with] so much history and visual beauty" needs to include "Native Americans and their contributions" (48:30) as well as their trials and tribulations. During the concluding minutes of his interview, he exhorts that "we don't forget" (52:35) about this period of American history.

Michael Dante's story is significant here if only because of his knowledge and ultimate recognition

---

[40] Dante's use of the adverb "possibly" is problematic if only because the history of genocide of Native Americans at the hands of "discovers" and their progeny dates back centuries. Paradoxical for sure as he bemoans the exclusion of "Native Americans and their contributions" to U.S. history. Among the many, one need only recall the Gnadenhutten Massacre of 1782, when 96 Native Americans were slaughtered two at a time by Delaware militiamen.

of the Native American's plight. Through his work as a professional actor, Dante has acquired an historical knowledge that seems to counter, in turn, an historical illiteracy among some who champion the sign /Columbus/ and all that it pertains. And while we may not know what Dante's thoughts are on Columbus, his desire to be fully informed about the history of Native Americans con only have a constructive impact in some manner or form.[41]

4. CELEBRATE, AND ENCOURAGE, the growing presence of Italian Americans within the world of philanthropy that began with the likes of OSIA (through its various *mutuo soccorso* societies) and Amadeo Giannini (the initial financier of Disney in the 1930s), and how current organizations and individuals such as — and there are more — the Columbus Citizens Foundation, the Giambelli Foundation, NIAF, the Tiro a Segno Club, UNICO, and others (I have in mind

---

[41] I have in mind, as one example of historical illiteracy, a statement made by the then national president of the Order Sons and Daughters of Italy in America. In reaction to the idea that in San Francisco Columbus Day would be shared with Indigenous People, and hence the day would be known as Italian Heritage Day / Indigenous People, Vera Girolami stated the following on the "Save Columbus Day" Facebook page: "We know what Italian Americans did for and in the City of San Francisco, what did Indigenous people do?" This statement was followed up by Giuseppina Venci: "Indigenous ppl did nothing for this Country. and still do nothing but to live under the Government benefits taking money and FS from taxes payers" (cited as written).

here the late Baroness Mariuccia Zerilli Mirimò and her $8 million that revolutionized Italian Studies at NYU) who have contributed millions of dollars to scholarships and to cultural and scientific (etymologically speaking, acquisition of knowledge) research projects.

Research and curricular matters underscore some of what Italian Americans as individuals and numerous organizations have supported; indeed, said research and curricula should be reconsidered and hence invested with the highest of socio-cultural currency within the well-heeled Italian/American associations. To be sure, it all needs to be more systematic with regard to the immediacy of need. For instance, I would contend that a first project for funding should be a concise history of Italians in America. It is true that there are a number of books available, one need only recall Maria Laurino's *The Italian Americans: A History*, which is a companion piece to the PBS series of the same title by John Maggio. A more ambitious venture would be to read Connell and Pugliese's *The Routledge History of Italian Americans*. But what I have in mind is something more basic than these two and others that have appeared over the years: a primer of sorts that offers a strict chronological history of the innumerable people and events that encompass what people are wont to call, "the Italian-American community"; and said history should begin with 1776.

Above all, moreover, is the urgent need for a national strategy that might surely include, and yet also go beyond, the Columbus Affair. The above-mentioned primer is a first step. We all need to be as best informed as we can of our history, culture, and present-day affairs. From there, we can then identify those areas that need not only further research but indeed a long-term plan of cultural awareness. Such a category of ideas and projects would constitute the organization of systematic research, if not the creation of the above-cited think tank.

Said organization of systematic research — again, read, think tank — should also have a fundamental goal of making sure Italian/American studies is included in college curricula. The scholars in question would study the initial geographical areas of need and in which colleges to begin (e.g., public or institutions), the subject matter of the first courses to be included, and eventually set up a series of courses that can be studied alongside various majors that run the gamut from economics, history, film, literature, sociology, anthropology, political science, and so on. At the same time, there needs to be an analogous strategy for K-12. A curriculum had been developed by a group of educators in New Jersey well over a decade or two ago; as excellent as it seemed at the time, it never spread beyond the local level for reasons unbeknownst today. In turn, a college curriculum was also developed by a committee of professors for the State of New York in 1989. Interdisciplinary in nature, and

hence intellectually inclusive, it was adopted sporad-
ically for professional development seminars, never
updated nor truly promoted beyond the proverbial
Tri-State Area.

What we at the John D. Calandra Italian American Institute have done is launch an international
professional development seminar in collaboration
with an Italian university on the Italian diaspora. First
held in Calabria, the Italian Diaspora Studies Summer Seminar (IDSSS) is a three-week professional
development curriculum for college faculty and
doctoral students held in collaboration with the Università degli Studi Roma Tre. It runs from Monday
through Thursday, approximately from 10:00 AM to
6:00 PM, with a break for lunch. Over the first five
years, we have had more than eighty participants,
all of whom received a fellowship to cover fifty percent of the program costs. The population, to date,
has been split between graduate students – at the
doctoral level for the most part – and professors,
the latter more numerous. The graduate students
also can earn as many as six graduate credits trans-
ferred to their home institutions.[42] In some cases, the
professors attending as fellows, in turn, have been
given release time from their home institutions and,
as well, funding to cover the other fifty percent of

---

[42] This is dependent entirely on the individual institution where
the graduate student is matriculated. Neither the IDSSS nor
Roma Tre University can guarantee which colleges and universities will decide the acceptance of credits.

the program costs. Further still, and this is one of the primary goals of the IDSSS, numerous faculty fellows have returned to their respective institutions and created and offered courses on various aspects of the Italian diaspora. The Seminar is funded primarily through grants and donations with administrative assistance from the John D. Calandra Italian American Institute and the Department of Foreign Languages, Literatures, and Cultures of the Università degli Studi Roma Tre.[43]

[43] For more information on the IDSSS, see my "Italian Diaspora Studies and the University: Professional Develop-ment and Curricular Matters" (2020a). Funders include the Francesco and Mary Giambelli Foundation, the Alexandra De Luise Private Gift, the Italian Language and Inter-Cultural Alliance (ILICA), CUNY's Office of Executive Vice Chancellor for Academic Affairs, as well as the National Italian American Foundation (NIAF), OSIA Grabnde Lodge of New York, UNICO National and UNICO Brookhaven, and the American Italian Educators Association (AIEA).

A PRESCRIPTION AND AN ANTIDOTE

I have outlined both a prescription and an antidote in a recent essay (2020a). There, I spoke to a therapeutic and recuperative challenge that involves at least seven components:

1. history
2. acculturation vs. assimilation
3. representation (yesterday and today)
4. articulation of ethnicity
5. identity
6. inter-ethnic collaboration
7. education

Another aspect of this challenge is that it possesses a double-layered consciousness: such awareness is distinguished by an "internal" and an "external" cognizance that are *de facto* dissimilar in origin but not in impact. All of this is ultimately negotiated through a constitutive act that is founded on pedagogy, tutelage, and reflection.

These seven components are the building blocks for us to arrive at a consciously analytical awareness of who we are and what our Italian and/or Italian/ American heritage is. In studying our "history" as best we can in its entirety, we come to see how Italian immigrants and their progeny evolved into that individual we know as an Italian American. We come to understand their trials and tribulations as well as their successes, a combination of events and phenomena that add to our own sense of self. How much of this heritage we decide to appropriate and recognize as ours will result in whether we engage in either "acculturation" or "assimilation." If we move more toward the former, then our heritage culture — sometimes referred to as a "minority" culture — succeeds in retaining those unique cultural signs such as language, food, customs, the arts (e.g., literature, cinema, painting, sculpture, etc.) and other behavioral patterns. If, instead, we tend toward the latter, then our heritage culture eventually loses all of it signs and markers that distinguish it as separate from the host — sometimes referred to as a "majority" culture; this includes the above-mentioned language, food, customs, and other behavioral patterns. At this juncture, then, one is an un*hyphenated* American, and that is fine; and his/her ethnic journey of discovery ends here.

However, in opting for acculturation, we eventually gain an awareness, a sensitivity as well, we might say (among numerous other things), of how we are represented, both yesterday and today, and how we might want to be represented tomorrow. As we become more familiar with the historical phenomena of our past and reconcile them with current cultural experiences, we gain a greater "Italian" consciousness and hence become more efficient in our "articulation of our ethnicity." We begin to develop, that is, an "identity" as a *hyphenated* American, or, better, an "Italian American."

This abbreviated description of an individual's passage to hyphenation leads to the last two components identified above: "inter-ethnic collaboration" and "education." The advantages of the former bring us to understand more fully the trials and tribulations of Native Americans and other immigrant groups as well, be it the loss of national sovereignty for Native Americans through genocide, or, of other U.S. ethnics' immigration, be it imposed or chosen (e.g., slavery or economic despair). Such acquisition of greater knowledge leads to an understanding that then affords us the possibility to gain a more complete — and, I would add, complex — awareness of our own overall experience and how it then relates to their respective experiences within the greater mosaic of what we know as the United States. It is, hence, at this juncture where we reach that level of education that grounds us more firmly in our "Italian-Americanness" and, one hopes, renders us empathetic with other causes as well.

But this seventh component of education, as I intend it here, does not figure only as the endpoint in one's development of his/her Italian-Americanness. It has yet another facet to it, one that exhibits a dual perspective that is analogous to the double-layered consciousness I mentioned above, one that is distinguished by an "internal" and an "external" cognizance. In fact, we saw above that education is an end point, the result of an acquisition of knowledge and insight vis-à-vis one's Italian-Americanness, one's ethnic identity; that is, his/her "internal" cognizance. With regard to an "external" cognition, in turn, education becomes a concerted, transitive operation of instructing or informing those who do not know, namely inducing knowledge of Italian/American history and culture to s/he who is uninformed. In turn, the same "internal" and "external" cognizance I mentioned above is now representative of the necessity to approach both populations, the Italian/American, which is "internal," and the non-Italian/American, which is "external." Our challenge as proponents of Italian/American culture, be we educators or heads of national ethnic voluntary associations and NGOs, is, to be sure, that as many people as possible are informed of and hence acquainted and conversant with the history of Italians in the United States.

NON-CONCLUSIVE THOUGHTS

I close with some thoughts that have their roots in other writings of mine, especially the first chapter of my *Re-reading Italian Americana*. What I do wish to state at this juncture is that it should be patently clear that some form of systematic research that goes beyond one issue, no matter how significant it may be, including the Columbus Affair, is a necessity too long absent. All the efforts expended on various and sundry issues by many different organizations — alas, many of them each on their own — can only propagate a balkanization of Italian Americans. As long as such a structure is not in place, any success at some sort of national discussion remains subverted by some form of nonpareil loyalty if not fealty to local organizations. The idea that we must all be on the same page, if not walking in goose step, is counterproductive and will only lead to an even greater division than some form of cohesion.[44]

---

[44] One example of this restrictive notion of "all on the same page or else" was evidenced in spring 2021. The Conference of Presidents of Major Italian American Organizations (COPOMIAO) had decided to join a lawsuit against the mayor of Philadelphia after he had made a unilateral decision to remove the Columbus statue from municipal property. When some members asked to see the brief so they could consult with their respective lawyers, the request was denied, and they were told that if they did not allow the inclusion in the brief of their organization's name and its representative to COPOMIAO, it would have to withdraw its membership. No if, ands, or buts! Thus, as of this writing, in addition to the departure of the John D. Calandra Italian American

Greater still, without a nationally coordinated system of research, there is the added risk of not being able to engage in and hence succeed with an efficacious teaching of the public at large. And so, it is incumbent upon all of us — leaders of Italian/American voluntary organizations, scholars and educators, potential philanthropists, and the like — to join forces — regardless of differences on single issues, even the Columbus Affair — and contribute to the creation of that long-awaited "think tank." If there is one thing that we have all learned, it is that we cannot always rely on the government for funding of these types of enterprises.[45]

Within this panoply of the four above-mentioned objectives discussed throughout, and the accompanying thoughts surrounding these and other goals, lies — some might say even squarely — Christopher Columbus. Again, as symbol, the sign /Columbus/ needs to be re-considered and re-examined — though not necessarily cast aside *in toto* and immediately banished to the scrap-pile of history — as

Institute, four other organizations withdrew: Giambelli Foundation, NIAF, National Organization of Italian American Women, Tiro a Segno.

[45] The John D. Calandra Italian American Institute in this sense was an anomaly to some degree. It was a time when we had a larger group of Italian/American public officials and private citizens on both the state and local levels who were very much engaged with their Italian/Americanness. They were very well informed of the history of discrimination against Italian Americans within The City University of New York, as the late state senator John D. Calandra had demonstrated (1978).

we move forward in this national debate. It is, I would contend, incumbent upon Italian Americans to discuss and debate the issue as a community unto itself first and foremost. But it is, as well, paramount that it be done in the most informed of manners.

I would submit that there are historical gaps on both sides of the aisle. There is much more research to be done, and much more rhetorical strategies need to be developed. Arguing for Columbus, according to this precept, makes one believe s/he is pitted against what s/he might characterize a *fashionable politically correct* thought process. In turn, arguing against Columbus, according to this second precept, makes one believe s/he is pitted against a *closed-minded conservative thought process* that does not take into account the Native-American's conceptual and visceral reaction to the Columbus legacy. In this regard, the anti-Columbus people might have the upper hand in this important debate. There is the historical record that amply demonstrates the four-plus centuries of suffering by Native Americans as a result of the two worlds being connected. That said, pro-Columbus people need to construct an historically fact-based argument that might counter this horrible aspect of the Columbus legacy, as we saw Anne Paolucci underscore above. They might succeed, in part, from the expertise of a scholar who can construct an historical, factual narrative that, in the end, is rhetorically persuasive to a significant degree; said scholar has yet to appear. They need to know the complete history (this also includes reading the likes of Francisco de Bobadilla and Bartolomé de las Casas) in order to make sense of it all and, perhaps, make the argument that people have made about Washington and Jefferson, two slave owners whose greater accomplishments — we all know what they are — seem to have saved them from the dumping ground of history. [47]

In the spirit of producing as exhaustive study as possible would be to begin with the *Repertorium Columbianum*, which is "a collection of contemporary sources relating to Columbus's four voyages, and the interpenetration of hitherto separate worlds that resulted from them. This multivolume series will provide in readily accessible form the basic documents that are the starting-point for research into this pivotal moment in world history; they form the indispensable tools for all scholarly enquiry into the encounter."[48]

As I mentioned at the outset of this crisscross of contrasting thoughts, in my role as Dean of the John D. Calandra Italian American Institute, I had offered

---

[47] I say to a significant degree because I am not sure if there will ever be 100% agreement, and we might have to accept that there are certain things about which we will simply not all concur.

With regard to a scholar coming forth, said person most likely may not without the respectful recognition of such work, as one would readily acknowledge for any of a number of other professions, especially those that exist outside the humanities.
[48] This is the description the publisher Brepols offers on its website of the ten books that make up its *Repertorium Columbianum*.

a semblance of a blueprint to some pro-Columbus people in summer 2020; it met notable silence. We also offered airtime to the newly formed group of pro-Columbus people, an invitation for them to discuss their *razon d'etre* and strategies for moving forward in support of Columbus.[49] After a couple of months of a pleasant back and forth with one of the group's representatives, nothing of substance ever came to fruition. Hence, we moved forward, and, to date, and have sponsored two live programs on Columbus via Zoom, one on July 27, 2020, entitled, "Columbus on Trial: Screening and Discussion"; the other on October 1, 2020, entitled, "Talking Columbus."[50] The July program was a discussion of the recent film, *Columbus on Trial*, by Marylou and Jerome Bongiorno.[51] Present with the filmmakers were pro-

---

[49] National Columbus Education Foundation was formed in mid-2020. Its website states: "The National Columbus Education Foundation was organized to develop policy solutions and proposals for the preservation of Columbus Day and to correct the false narrative surrounding Columbus. We will promote active discussion on his accomplishments, and why Columbus Day should be celebrated by all Americans." See its website (https://knowcolumbus.org)for more information.

[50] See Works Cited for the URLs to each of these programs.

[51] *Columbus on Trial* is an extremely well researched film on the Columbus controversy. Through an interrogation of the ghost of Christopher Columbus by the ghost of 18th-century American political activist Elizabeth Willing Powel (a confidante of President George Washington), we as viewers witness a 21st-century argument over controversies surrounding Columbus's discovery of the New World. Extremely well researched and presented as a docudrama, the film leaves the viewer to decide. Further

fessors Fred Gardaphé and Leslie Wilson; I was the moderator. On October 1, in turn, I again moderated a discussion with professors William Connell, Fred Gardaphé, Laura Ruberto, Joseph Sciorra, and Leslie Wilson.[52]

While there are those on both ends of the spectrum who have dug in their heels and, so it seems, will not entertain any notion of a discussion, there are instead others who will. I was delightfully surprised to hear as much in mid-October of 2020. On October 13, in fact, NIAF sponsored an on-line program entitled "Christopher Columbus and the National Debate." The program was described as follows:

> The National Italian American Foundation invites you to sit down with our panel of experts as we discuss the debate over the celebration of Christopher Columbus and his legacy in America. Our panelists, George Bochetto, William J. Connell, and Anthony C. Wisniewski will break down the history behind establishing Columbus Day, what it means not only to the Italian American community but other communities, and tackle the national debate on whether or not the statues should stay or go.

---

still, it may also serve as a blueprint for either side of the argument through a follow-up on the material presented therein.
[52] These two programs were to be the bookends to two other discussions: one with a group of young Italian Americans who are anti-Columbus; the third was to be with the NCEF, in order to have a cycle of programs representative of both sides.

The program ended on a positive note insofar as it left the question open ended. While Columbus was neither exalted to the heavens nor summarily thrown onto the dumping ground of history, he was, at least, contextualized for the moment. The ending of the cablecast went as follows:

ANTHONY C. WISNIEWSKI: Min. 52:08
There is a deficit in the level of American history being taught in this country today.... We could probably do a better job of that. As far as this particular aspect of history, I think it is pretty important that we do so for Christopher Columbus. ... NIAF and other related groups can be a great force of good, and again, providing an equal reasonable, historical explanation within context of what happened 530 or so years ago and how that has eventually, through its highs and lows of world and later-American history, brought us to where we are today. I think there are a lot more highs than lows. But the story needs to be told, because if the story isn't told, then you leave it to others to tell, that may be telling the story not from a position of strength or knowledge....

WILLIAM J. CONNELL: Professor, Seton Hall University: Min. 53:29
Back again to the question of why Columbus became so important, and it's because he captured the people's imagination. If you read his journals, crossing the Atlantic, finding these new places, it's

still remarkable and jaw-dropping to read his descriptions. And that's what needed going forward, thought, capturing people's imagination, not defending old stone monuments so much as projecting people into the future. There are good books for instance for Italian Americans to read, read Gay Talese, Don DeLillo, John Fante, Diane di Prima, there's a big forward-looking educational project that I think can capture lots [inaudible] and can really build an imaginative world going forward that can comprise Columbus quite easily. So instead of circling the wagons, instead of being defensive, embrace, and this is the message of tolerance that Anthony was also bringing forward, let's look to the future instead of fighting about things that happened 500 years ago.

GABRIELLA MILETI, Director of Special Programs: Min. 55:45
[Our panelists] have mentioned a couple of resources, so we are going to compile those resources and send them to you the viewer along with the recording of tonight's show so we can educate ourselves to be more aware of what we're talking about when people bring up the topic of Columbus Day and Christopher Columbus, as a whole.

ANTHONY DISANDRO, member, NIAF Board of Directors: Min. 56:30
We probably needed another couple of hours on this topic to kind of walk through everything.

The open-ended *pause* to this program — I would
consider it as such to one of other chapters (read, discussions) to follow — and thus not an ending, did not
offer a definitive response to the conundrum of /Co-
lumbus/ and all that it pertains as a sign; it did not
establish whether the statues should stay or go. And
this is not necessarily a bad thing, precisely because,
as the panelists themselves stated, there continues "a
deficit in the level of American history being taught
in this country today" (Wisniewski); and, further still,
what is needed to move forward, according to Connell includes "thought, capturing people's imagination, not defending old stone monuments so much as
projecting people into the future. There are good
books for instance for Italian Americans to read, read
Gay Talese, Don DeLillo, John Fante, Diane di Prima,
there's a big forward-looking educational project that
I think can capture lots [inaudible] and can really
build an imaginative world going forward that can
comprise Columbus quite easily" (53:29).

   We need to return to — if not access for the first
time — those books and archives that can furnish us
with the information necessary for our individual
historical foundation of the Italian immigrant experience in the United States; we need to "educate ourselves to be more aware of what we're talking about
when people bring up the topic of Columbus Day
and Christopher Columbus, as a whole" (Mileti). We
can no longer rely on familial anecdotes and stories
— some true, some not — passed down from one

generation to the next. Memory steeped in nostalgia can only fog things up; it can only lead us to apocryphal sayings that have no historical fact: e.g., the faux notion that Italians came to the United States because they wanted to become Americans and learn English is debunked by the fact that during the great wave of immigration (1880-1924) close to 50% of the 4,200,000 Italian immigrants returned to Italy. "It is an uncomfortable history," as one of the Native Americans in *Columbus Day Legacy* states (Blain, 5:19). Indeed! And not only is the history of the Columbus factor uncomfortable, so too is the highly multi-faceted, complex history of the Italian in the United States; knowledge of the latter will surely impact reception of the former.

In the long run, as Connell and Gardaphé have stated, Columbus will always be with us, or so it seems. It will literally take an act of Congress to eliminate Columbus Day. Nonetheless, we must also acknowledge a tidal wave of anti-Columbus manifestations within the past three-plus years especially, unprecedented even compared to the reactions to celebrations of Columbus during the quincentenary in 1992. As Joseph Sciorra has pointed out (2021), as the national holiday was a result of Columbus Day being created at local and state levels, it is not unimaginable that the same could happen in reverse.

Speaking indeed of Congress and other elected and appointed officials as well, let us close, for now, with the following interrogatives: Where are the national Italian/American elected officials and government officers? Where are the likes of Michael Pompeo, Kenneth Cuccinelli, Stephen Scalise, Nancy Pelosi, Joseph Manchin, Michael Enzi, Tim Ryan, and others to engage in any and/or many of the issues that Italian Americans face?[54] Rest assured that other ethnic/racial groups have a greater, direct line to their government representatives for their respective claims and petitions. We Italian Americans seem to be woefully deficient in this socio-cultural phenomenon that has, at its base, a political underpinning. This is surely a sore lack in a culture that is the legacy of Catherine of Siena and Elena Cornaro Piscopia up to Antonio Gramsci, Rosa Braidotti, and Umberto Eco, not to mentioned all those in between, especially with specific regard to the Renaissance (e.g., Niccolò Machiavelli and Giordano Bruno) and the Italian period of Enlightenment (e.g., Cesare Beccaria and Giambattista Vico), from Italy, and from the United States, the social, intellectual, political, and cultural thought processes of those from Carlo Tresca, Arturo Giovannitti, Luigi Antonini, Frances Winwar, Vito Marcantonio, Angela Bambace, Ella Grasso, and Mary Sansone, to more recent voices of Joseph Tusiani, Lucia Chiavola Birnbaum, Robert Viscusi, Donna Lopiano, Robert Orsi, and Donna Gabaccia, to name a few.

---

[54] I dare muse, as I list such names, how much of our history any and all of these and other Italian Americans have studied, and what do they know.

WORKS CITED

Alexander VI, Pope. 1493. "Demarcation Bull." May 4. The Gilder Lehrman Collection, GLC04093. www. gilderlehrman.org.

Alvarez, Angel Rodriguez. 2008. *Mitologia Taina o Eyeri Ramon Pane y La Relacion Sobre LasAntiguedades de los Indios*. San Juan, P.R.: Editorial Nuevo Mundo.

Anonymous. 2017. "Harlem Speaker Melissa Mark-Viverito and Others Rally to Remove Offensive Statue." *Harlem World Magazine*. August 21. https://www.harlemworldmagazine.com/harlem-speaker-melissa-mark-viverito-others-rally-remove-offensive-statue/. Accessed August 1, 2020.

Battisti, Danielle. 2019. *'Whom We Shall Welcome': Italian Americans and Immigration Reform 1945–1965*. New York: Fordham University Press.

Bergreen, Lawrence. 2011. *Columbus: The Four Voyages, 1492-1504*. New York: Viking.

Bradley, Carol J. 1990. "Towards a Celebration: The Columbus Monument in New York," in *Italian Americans Celebrate Life. The Arts and Popular Culture*, eds. Paola A. Sensi-Isolani and Anthony Julian Tamburri (Staten Island, NY: American Italian Historical Association) 81-94.

Brown, Dee. 1970. *Bury My Heart at Wounded Knee*. New York: Holt, Rinehart & Winston.

Calandra, John D. 1978. *A History of Italian-American Discrimination at CUNY*. Albany, NY: New York State Senate.

Catholic Church. Pope. 1868. *Bullarium patronatus Portugalliæ regum in ecclesiis Africæ, Asiæ atque Oceaniæ bullas, brevia, epistolas, decreta, actaque sanctæ sedis ab Alexandro III ad hoc usque tempus amplectens.* Volumes 1-3. Levy Maria Jordão Paiva Manso (visconde de), ed. Portugal: Ex typographia nationali.

Cerulli, Stephen. 2019. *Italian/Americans and the American Racial System: Contadini to Settler Colonists?* The Graduate Center, City University of New York. https://academicworks.cuny.edu/gc_etds/3178/. Accessed July 21, 2020.

"Christopher Columbus & the National Debate." 2020. National Italian American Foundation. October 13. https://www.youtube.com/watch?v=fFeoWrkY6Kk&t=619s.

Cliff, Nigel. 2012. *The Last Crusade: The Epic Voyages of Vasco da Gama.* New York: HarperCollins.

"Columbus on Trial: Screening and Discussion." 2020. July 27. https://www.youtube.com/watch?v=uFcofK9XWTg.

Connell, William J. 2020. "George Floyd and ... Columbus? The Twin 'Original Sins' of the Conquest of America." La Voce di New York. June 12. https://www.lavocedinewyork.com/en/news/2020/06/12/george-floyd-and-columbus-the-twin-original-sins-of-the-conquest-of-america/. Accessed June 30, 2020.

Connell, William J. 2018. "Italians in the Early Altantic World," in *The Routledge History of Italian Americans.*

William J. Connell and Stanislao G. Pugliese, eds. New York: Routledge, 2018.

Connell, William J. 2013. "Who's Afraid of Columbus?" *Italian Americana* 31.2 (Spring): 136-147.

Connell, William J. and Stanislao G. Pugliese, eds. 2018. *The Routledge History of Italian Americans.* New York: Routledge.

Columbus, Christopher. 1893. "Journal of the First Voyage of Columbus," in *Journal of Christopher Columbus (during his first voyage, 1492-93), and Documents Relating to the Voyages of John Cabot and Gaspar Corte Real.* Clements R. Markham, ed. London: Hakluyt Society. 15-193.

Columbus Day Legacy. 2011. Bennie Klain, Dir. Trickster Films and Native American Public Communications.

Columbus on Trial. 2020. Marylou and Jerome Bongiorno. Bongiorno Productions.

Dante, Michael. 2017. *Winterhawk's Land.* Albany, GA: BearManor Media.Delaney, Carol. 2011. *Columbus and the Quest for Jerusalem: How Religion Drove the Voyages that Led to America.* New York: Free Press.

Delany, Carol. 2011.*Columbus and the Quest for Jerusalem.* New York: Free Press.

Deschamps, Bénédicte. 2015. "'The cornerstone is laid': Italian American Memorial Building in New York City and Immigrants' Right to the City at the Turn of the Twentieth Century." *European Journal of American studies* 10-3. URL: http://journals.open edition.org/ejas/11299.

Deschamps, Bénédicte. 2001. "Italian-Americans and Columbus Day: A Quest for Consensus Between National and Group Identities, 1840–1910." In *Celebrating Ethnicity and Nation: American Festive Culture from the Revolution to the Early Twentieth Century.* Edited by J. Heideking, G. Fabre, & K. Dreisbach. New York: Berghahn Books. 124–139.

Doctrine of Discovery: A Timeline. N.D. Saint Paul Interfaith Network.

Duggan, Kevin. 2020. "Civic Gurus Call For Removal Of Downtown Brooklyn Columbus Statue," *Brooklyn Paper.* December 10. https://www.brook lynpaper.com/downtown-brooklyn-columbus-statue-removal/. Accessed December 11, 2020.

Emerson, Ralph Waldo. 1950. *The Complete Essays and Other Writings of Ralph Waldo Emerson.* Edited by Brooksß Atkinson, Forward by Tremaine Mc-Dowell. New York: Random House.

Hunter, Douglas. 2011. *The Race to the New World: Christopher Columbus, John Cabot, and a Lost History of Discovery.* New York: Palgrave MacMillan.

Fernández-Armesto, Felipe. 2011. "Faulty Navigators: Seeking to revolutionize views of the Age of Exploration, four books instead reveal more about the state of popular history." *Wall Street Journal.* September 17. https://online.wsj.com/article/SB 10001424053111904836104576558540795723736.ht ml. Accessed September 15, 2020.

Fernández-Armesto, Felipe. 2010a. *1492: The Year the World Began.* New York: HarperOne.

Fernández-Armesto, Felipe. 2010b *Columbus on Himself*. New York: Hackett Publishing Company.

Fernández-Armesto, Felipe. 2007. *Pathfinders: A Global History of Exploration*. New York: W. W. Norton.

Fernández-Armesto, Felipe. 1991. *Columbus*. New York: Oxford University Press.

Fleegler Jr. Robert. 2015. *Ellis Island Nation. Immigration Policy and American Identity in the Twentieth Century*. Philadelphia: University of Pennsylvania Press.

Frichner, Tonya Gonnella. 2010. "Preliminary study of the impact on indigenous peoples of the international legal construct known as the Doctrine of Discovery." United Nations Economic and Social Council. E /C.19/2010/13.

Gardaphé, Fred. 2020. "Beyond Columbus: An Italian American Wake Up Call." *i-Italy.org*. July 27. https://www.iitaly.org/magazine/focus/op-eds/article/beyond-columbus-italian-american-wake-call. Accessed July 27, 2020.

Graham, Mike L. No date. "United Native America Working with Italian Americans To Bring About the End of Columbus Day in America." http://www.unitednativeamerica.com/letters/Italian_Americans.html. Accessed January 30, 2021.

Guglielmo, Jennifer and Salvatore Salerno. 2003. *Are Italians White? How Race is Made in America*. New York: Routledge, 2003.

Johnson vs. McInstosh. 1823. Supreme Court of the United States.

Harlan, Jennifer. 2019. "Overlooked No More: Emma Stebbins, Who Sculpted an Angel of New York," New York Times, May 29. https://www.nytimes.com/2019/05/29/obituaries/emma-stebbins-overlooked.html. Accessed December 11, 2020.

Jackson, Jessica Barbata. 2020. *Dixie's Italians: Sicilians, Race, and Citizenship in the Jim Crow Gulf South.* Baton Rouge, LA: Lousiana State University Press.

Kubal, Timothy. 2009. *Cultural Movements and Collective Memory: Christopher Columbus and the Rewriting of the National Origin Myth.* New York: Palgrave.

Laurino, Maria. 2014. *The Italian Americans: A History.* New York: Norton.

Luconi, Stefano. 2012. "Columbus and Vespucci as Italian Navigators: The Ethnic Legacy of Explorations and Italian Americans' Search for Legitimacy in the United States." In *Florence in Italy and Abroad from Vespucci to Contemporary Innovators.* Florence: Florence Campus Publishing House. 62-77.

Nevaer, Louis. 2020. "The Lynching That Gave Us Columbus Day." Medium. June 18. https://medium.com/@nevaer1/the-lynching-that-gave-us-columbus-day-eb5179b01aca. Accessed August 1, 2020.

Nicolas V, Pope. 1452. "Nicolaus Episcopus," in *Bellarium Patronatus Portugalliae Regum in Ecclesiis Afriace, Asiae, Atque Oceaniae.* Vol. 1. Levy Maria Jordao, ed. Olisipone: Ex Typographia Nationali, 1868.

Ortiz, Rafael. 2021. "Book Review on the Bobadilla's Report." *Official: Christopher Columbus.* http://www.

officialchristophercolumbus.com/. Accessed June 14, 2021.

Page, Clarence. 1991. "Columbus a Demon or Saint? Depends." *Chicago Tribune.* https://www.chicago tribune.com/news/ct-xpm-1991-10-09-9104010355-story.html. Accessed August 1, 2020.

Paolucci, Anne. 2007. "Preserving the Future Through The Past (A Personal Assessment)." In *Italian-American Perspectives.* New York: Griffon House.

Repertorium Columbianum. 198-2004. L. Formisano, G. Symcox, B. Sullivan, General Editors. http://www.brepols.net/Pages/BrowseBySeries.aspx?Tr eeSeries=RC.

Robertson, Ed. 2017. "Interview with Michael Dante." *TV Confidential.* Show No. 370. July 11. https://www.youtube.com/watch?v=q5moJumcqNc.

Rose, Brent. 2012. "Neil deGrasse Tyson: Columbus Landing in America Was the Most Important Event in Human History." Gizmodo. https://gizmodo.com/neil-degrasse-tyson-columbus-landing-in-america-was-th-5928576. Accessed August 1, 2020.

Ruberto, Laura E. and Joseph Sciorra. 2020. "'Columbus Might Be Dwarfed to Obscurity': Italian Americans' Engagement with Columbus Monuments in a Time of Decolonization." In *Public Memory in the Context of Transnational Migration and Displacement.* Edited by Marschall S. New York: Palgrave Macmillan. 61-93.

Sague Jr, Miguel. 2008. "New Evidence Concenring Columbus's Exploitation of Tainos." *Indigenous Caribbean Network*. https://indigenouscaribbean. ning.com/profiles/blogs/new-evidence-concern ing. Accessed June 14, 2021.

Salvetti, Patrizia. 2017 [2012]. *Rope and Soap. Lynchings of Italians in the United States*. New York: Bordighera Press.

Santoro, Vincenzina. 2017. "Why Hate Eradicators Should Reconsider the Removal of Christopher Columbus Statues." https://www.intellectual takeout.org/article/why-hate-eradicators-should-reconsider-removal-christopher-columbus-statues/, September 5. Accessed August 1, 2020.

"Save Columbus Day" FaceBook. https://www. facebook.com/groups/savecolumbusday/permal ink/363708640775774. Accessed March 4, 2018.

Sciorra, Joseph. 2021. Private Conversation with Anthony Julian Tamburri. February 7.

"Talking Columbus." 2020. October 1. https://www. youtube.com/watch?v=lxKSuhZ Akp4. Accessed October 3, 2020.

Tamburri, Anthony Julian. 2020a. "Italian Diaspora Studies and the University: Professional Development and Curricular Matters" in *This Hope Sustains the Scholar: Essays in Tribute to the Work of Robert Viscusi*. Siân Gibby, Joseph Sciorra, Anthony Julian Tamburri, eds. New York: Bordighera Press.

Tamburri, Anthony Julian. 2020b. "The Semiotics of Labeling. 'Italian' to 'American,' 'Non-white' to 'White,' and Other Privileges of Choosing." In *Circolazione di persone e di idee. Integrazione ed esclusione tra Europa e Americhe*. Sabrina Vellucci and Susanna Nanni, eds. New York: Bordighera Press.

Tamburri, Anthony Julian. 2020c. "Public Monuments and Indro Montanelli: A Case of Misdirected Reverence?" in https://www.lavocedinewyork.com/en/news/2020/06/24/public-monuments-and-indro-montanelli-a-case-of-misdirected-reverence/.

Tamburri, Anthony Julian. 2018. "The Making of America; and Italians Need Apply! Just Ask Carnegie Hall" in https://www.lavocedinewyork.com/en/new-york/2018/01/27/the-making-of-america-and-italians-need-apply-just-ask-carnegie-hall/.

Tamburri, Anthony Julian. 2017a. "When We Were the Muslims: President Trump's Executive Order and the immigrant history of my grandmother" in https://www.lavocedinewyork.com/en/news/2017/01/29/when-we-were-the-muslims/.

Tamburri, Anthony Julian. 2017b. "'…And There Was No One Left to Speak for Me'" in https://www.lavocedinewyork.com/en/news/2017/08/21/and-there-was-no-one-left-to-speak-for-me/.

Tamburri, Anthony Julian. 2017c. "The Columbus Controversy and the Politics of Omission." *La Voce di New York*. December 17. https://www.lavocedinew

york.com/en/new-york/2017/12/17/the-columbus-controversy-and-the-politics-of-omission/.

Tamburri, Anthony Julian. 2016. "The Coincidence of Italian Cultural Hegemonic Privilege and the Historical Amnesia of Italian Diaspora Articulations" in http://bloggers.iitaly.org/bloggers/40665/coincidence-italian-cultural-hegemonic-privilege-and-historical-amnesia-italian-diasp.

Tamburri, Anthony Julian. 2014a. *Re-reading Italian Americana: Generalities and Specificities on Literature and Criticism.* Madison, NJ: Fairleigh Dickinson UP, 2014.

Tamburri, Anthony Julian. 2014b. "Silence is not always golden..." in http:// bloggers.iitaly.org/bloggers/38457/silence-not-always-golden.

Tamburri, Anthony Julian. 2013a. Things that make you go hmmm..." in http://bloggers.iitaly.org/bloggers/37120/things-make-you-go-hmmm.

Tamburri, Anthony Julian. 2013b. "Elected Officials and The College Professor: Perspectives on Questions of Human Values" in http://bloggers.iitaly.org/bloggers/36625/elected-officials-and-college-professor-perspectives-questions-human-values.

Tamburri, Anthony Julian. 2013c. "Italy's PM recognizes historical discrimination against Italian immigrant in the US!" in http://bloggers.iitaly.org/bloggers/36008/italys-pm-recognizes-historical-discrimination-against-italian-immigrant-us.

Tamburri, Anthony Julian. 2013d. "Really? This is Section A news for the United States?" in http://bloggers.iitaly.org/bloggers/35643/really-section-news-united-states.

Tamburri, Anthony Julian. 2012a. "We Didn't Come Over on the Mayflower!" in http://bloggers.iitaly.org/bloggers/19107/we-didn-t-come-over-mayflower.

Tamburri, Anthony Julian. 2012b. "Roberto Saviano and the Problems of Italian America" in http://bloggers.iitaly.org/bloggers/18933/roberto-saviano-and-problems-italian-america.

Tamburri, Anthony Julian. 2011. "Is it possible that we just can't help ourselves?" in http://bloggers.iitaly.org/bloggers/18135/it-possible-we-just-cant-help-ourselves.

Tamburri, Anthony Julian. 2010a. Arizona Ethnic Studies Bill and Then Some..." in http://bloggers.iitaly.org/bloggers/14247/arizona-ethnic-studies-bill-and-then-some.

Tamburri, Anthony Julian. 2010b. "The Italian/American Writer in "Exile": At Home, Abroad, Wherever!" In *The Hyphenate Writer and The Legacy of Exile*. Paolo Giordano, ed. New York: Bordighera Press. 1-25.

Tamburri, Anthony Julian. 2009. "Just when we thought it was safe to go back into the water..." in http://bloggers.iitaly.org/bloggers/7664/just-when-we-thought-it-was-safe-go-back-water

Tamburri, Anthony Julian. 2008. "An Offer We Can Refuse" in http://bloggers.iitaly.org/bloggers/4232/offer-we-can-refuse.

Tamburri, Anthony Julian. 2007. "Bigotry" in http://bloggers.iitaly.org/bloggers/560/bigotry.

Tamburri, Anthony Julian. 2006. "Second Thoughts on the 'Diasporic' Culture of Italians in America: Here, There, Wherever." *Italica* 83. 3/4 (Fall-Winter, 2006): 720-728.

Tamburri, Anthony Julian. 1991. *To Hyphenate or not to Hyphenate: the Italian/American Writer: Or, An* Other *American?* Montreal: Guernica Editions.

Vallillo, John and Pam Dorazio Dean. 2020. "Akron Changes Name of Columbus Day to Italian American Heritage and Culture Day." *La gazzetta italiana.* August. https://www.lagazzettaitaliana.com/history-culture/9489-akron-changes-name-of-columbus-day-to-italian-american-heritage-and-culture-day. Accessed August 1, 2020.

Varela, Consuelo. 2006. *La caída de Cristóbol Colón. El juicio de Bobadilla.* Edición y transcripción de Isabel Aguirre. Madrid: Marcel Pons Historia.

Viscusi, Robert. 2006. *Buried Caesars and Other Secrets of Italian American Writing.* Albany, NY: SUNY Press.

Vellon, Peter G. 2014. *A Great Conspiracy against Our Race: Italian Immigrant Newspapers and the Construction of Whiteness in the Early 20th Century.* New York: New York University Press.

Webb, Clive. 2002. "The Lynching of Siclian Immigrants in the Americans South, 1886-1910. *American Nineteenth Century History* 31.1 (2002): 45-76.

Wisniewski, Anthony C. 2020. "Columbus statues need context, not disrespect and desecration." *Ames Tribune.* July 1. https://www.amestrib.com/story/opinion/columns/2020/07/01/anthony-c-wisniewski-columbus-statues-need-context-not-disrespect-and-desecration/42034631/. Accessed, October 14, 2020.

White, Haden. 1973. "Interpretation in History." *New Literary History.* On Interpretation: II. 4.2 (Winter): 281-314.

Zavarzadeh, Mas'ud and Donald Morton. 1991. *Theory, (Post)Modernity Opposition. An "Other" Introduction to Literary and Cultural Theory.* Washington D.C.: Maisonneuve P.

Index of Names

Lopiano, Donna 79
Luconi, Stefano 25n12

Machiavelli, Niccolò 56, 79
Manchin, Joseph 79
Marcantonio, Vito 79
Mark-Viverito, Melissa 42-43
Martin, Dean 57
Means, Russell 35-37, 38, 56
Mileti, Gabriella 76-78
Morton, Donald 13n3, 21n8, 21-22
Mussolini, Benito 54n33

National Columbus Education Foundation 73n48
National Italian American Foundation (see also NIAF) 24n11, 61, 64n41, 69n44, 74-76
National Organization of Italian American Women 69n44
Nevaer, Louis 25

Order Sons and Daughters of America (see also OSIA) 24n11, 60, 64n11
Orsi, Robert 79
Ortiz, Rafael 32

Page, Clarence 17-18
Paolucci, Anne 8-9, 39-41, 41n23
Patri, Angelo 57
Peirce, Charles Sanders 23-24
Pelosi, Nancy 79
Pierce, Charles B. 58
Pompeo, Micheal 79
Pope Alexander VI 50-51
Pope Nicholas V 49-50
Pugliese, Stanislao G. 7n1, 61-62

Repertorium Columbianum 72n47, 72
Robertson, Ed 59
Rose, Brent 34
Ruberto, Laura E. 8-9, 17n5, 19, 20-21, 22, 23n10, 45-46, 73
Ryan, Tim 79

Sague Jr, Miguel 32n19, 32-33
Salerno, Salvatore 29
Salvetti, Patrizia 25n12

NOTES

NOTES

ABOUT THE AUTHOR

ANTHONY JULIAN TAMBURRI is Distinguished Professor of European Languages and Literatures and Dean of the John D. Calandra Italian American Institute of Queens College, The City University of New York.

In addition to his numerous books and more than 120 essays and book chapters, he has edited close to thirty volumes. With Paolo A. Giordano and Fred L. Gardaphé, he is contributing co-editor of the volume *From The Margin: Writings in Italian Americana* (1991; 2nd edition, 2000), and co-founder of Bordighera Press, publisher of *Voices in Italian Americana, Italiana,* and four book series, and the LAURA/FRASCA POETRY PRIZE. Other edited volumes include, *Beyond the Margin: Readings in Italian Americana* (1998) and *Screening Ethnicity: Cinematographic Representations of Italian Americans in the United States* (2002).

His degrees are from Southern Connecticut State University (BS, Italian & Spanish), Middlebury College (MA, Italian), U.C. Berkeley (PhD, Italian & Spanish). He first taught in high-school, and subsequently moved on to Smith College, Middlebury College, Auburn University, and Purdue University, before moving to Florida Atlantic University where he served as Chair of Languages and Linguistics, then Associate Dean for Research, Graduate, and Interdisciplinary Studies, and director of the Ph.D. in Comparative Studies, before coming to The City University of New York.

Tamburri is past president of the American Italian Historical Association (now Italian American Studies Association) and the American Association of Teachers of Italian. He is executive producer of the TV program *Italics.* Among his honors, he was named Distinguished Alumnus in 2000 by Southern Connecticut State University; in 2008, then Bronx President Adolfo Carrion awarded him the Certificate of Appreciation for work as educator and community leader for Italian Americans; and, in 2010 he was conferred the honor of *Cavaliere dell'Ordine al Merito della Repubblica Italiana*. He received the "Frank Stella Person of the Year Award," ILICA. Other awards include: "The Lehman-LaGuardia Award for Civic Achievement." Commission for Social Justice Order Sons of Italy (New York State) in America and B'nai B'rith International (Metro-North Region) (2011); the AATI Award for Distinguished Service for Colleges and Universities (2013); the "Leonard Covello Award for Distinguished Service" of the Italian Teachers Association of New York (2013); The Joseph Coccia Jr. Heritage, Language and Culture Award exceptional efforts by word and deed in promoting and preserving our Italian Heritage, Language or Culture. UNICO National (2016); National Council of Columbia Associations, "Man of The Year" Award (2017).

ALSO BY ANTHONY JULIAN TAMBURRI

Praise for Tamburri's work:

I welcome Tamburri's contribution [*To Hyphenate or Not to Hyphenate* (1991)] to Italian Americans' ethnogenesis as co-creators of mainstream or alternative culture. He is working in his critical/intellectual way toward a vision of our culture that is coherent and harmonious not with its history of genocide, bigotry, racism, institutional violence, elitism and vicious socioeconomic competition, but with other values Sacco and Vanzetti came to America to actualize.

— Justin Vitiello, *Italica*

Per una lettura retrospettiva [1994] represents another important contribution by Tamburri to Palazzeschian studies. This new rereading of the Florentine writer's early works serves as valuable resource to scholars of Avant-gardism and Modernism. The author's familiarity with major theoretical and literary issues surrounding non-canonical writings helps reinforce the position of Palazzeschi as an avant-garde of international standing.

— Mark Pietralunga, *Italica*

[In *A Semiotic of Ethnicity* (1998)] Tamburri brings to the discussion of multiculturalism and Italian/American writing a familiarity with major critical currents at play in the field as well as a command of critical theory. His introduction of cognitive processing and consciousness are valuable additions to Italian/American studies in particular and ethnic studies in general. [...] Tamburri persuasively argues, "ethnicity is not a fixed essence passed down from one generation to the next" (14).

— Josephine Gattuso Hendin, *American Literary History*

Indeed, [*Re-Viewing Italian Americana* (2011)] is what the study of cinematic and other representations of Italian Americans should always aspire to achieve. Tamburri reminds us that, in continuing to face the challenge of making Italian/American studies a truly viable category, the scholar's task is to disseminate and transmit the culture in new ways. The contribution of this volume accomplishes just this. The rest of us are poised to follow Tarnburn's recommendation, and the example of the many scholars he cites, to take our culture more seriously.

—Tina Chiappetta-Miller, *Italian Culture*

Few scholars have contributed as much to the field of Italian-American Studies as Anthony Julian Tamburri. In his many books and essays, Tamburri has worked to establish Italian Americana as a valued topic of academic inquiry, and the scholars who contribute to the field today owe a debt of gratitude to him and his work. In his latest book, *Re-Viewing Italian Americana*, Tamburri once again challenges those interested in Italian Americans (not just scholars but also activists, students, and other related parties) to create a more inclusive and comprehensive picture of the myriad ways Italian-American ethnicity is represented cinematically and televisually, how it is used rhetorically, and how it is understood culturally.

— Jonathan J. Cavallero, *AltreItalie*

A few times—a very few times—in a generation, a work of literary and cultural scholarship, critical analysis, and winning polemic comes along that we confidently describe as a landmark in the field. For many reasons, *Re-Reading Italian Americana* [2014] qualifies for the honor. It is unique in its accessibility of presentation without sacrifice of precision and complexity, and tough in its call for Italian Americans to get involved, stop the cheerleading and sentimentality, and contribute.

—Frank Lentricchia

Anthony Julian Tamburri's [*Signing Italian/American Cinema* (2021)] will change the way you look at movies. Whether you study the form, teach cinema or watch for enjoyment, there is a rich garden of ideas in these essays that will challenge and delight you. Dr. Tamburri is one of the leading Italian American voices of our times. You will savor this collection. It's an intellectual Moviola by a man who knows movies.

—Adriana Trigiani, *The Shoemaker's Wife*

SPUNTINI

This book series is dedicated to the long essay. It includes those studies that are longer than the traditional journal-length essay and yet shorter than the traditional book-length manuscript. Intellectually, it is a light meal, a snack of sorts that holds you over for the full helping that comes with either lunch or dinner.

Anthony Julian Tamburri. *The Columbus Affair: Imperatives for an Italian American Agenda.* Volume 1. ISBN 978-1-955995-00-9

CPSIA information can be obtained
at www.ICGtesting.com
Printed in the USA
LVHW020058170821
695429LV00004B/101